Heinrich to Henry
A True World War II Story

By Marie Kramer
as told by Henry Cramer

Best wishes!
Marie Kramer
402-362-4357

Copyright 1997 by Marie Kramer
First Edition
All rights reserved
Printed in the United States of America

ISBN 0-9637525-4-5

To order copies contact the author/publisher:
Marie Kramer
York Mobile Plaza # 20
York, Nebraska 68467
See page 92 for more information.

Printed by
Service Press
Henderson, Nebraska 68371

*Dedicated
with sincere gratitude
to all the people
who made me feel
welcome
when I came
to the United States
of America.*

--Henry Cramer

Contents

Part I Heinrich

1. Our New Leader 7
2. Life in Germany 17
3. Into Battle 25
4. Moving Westward 37
5. On the Ship 47
6. A Civilian Again 53

Part II Henry

7. Behind the Windbreak 61
8. Esther 71
9. Life Goes On 85

Part One
Heinrich

1
Our New Leader

    The air was heavy with the sweet, enticing odor of chocolate and the spicy aroma of freshly baked cookies. We children, orderly and regimented, could scarcely contain our excitement as we filed through the door. Usually, such treats as chocolate milk and cookies were reserved for major holidays. How wonderful that the new German leader had proclaimed his birthday, April 20, as a holiday, and had provided this mouth-watering treat for us. All schools had been dismissed early, and the teachers had brought us to a community center for the celebration.
    When we were inside, the teacher directed us to face the picture that dominated one wall. On signal, we raised our right hands in salute. The air reverberated with the intensity of our simultaneous shout: "Heil Hitler!"
    We all agreed as we consumed our treat that Hitler was a great and wonderful man.

    Every segment of the community was organized, including the women who at that time were mainly homemakers. My mother Hinrike (Bless) Cramer, whose nickname was Rike (pronounced Reek-eh) returned from a political meeting one evening.
    "Everything we discussed pertained to our everyday lives," she told us. "Our motto is taken from the Bible. It is 'Faith, hope, and love!' from Corinthians. We were praised for being the mothers of the Fatherland, and

everyone who had three children or more was honored as a 'child-rich family'. Also, they said we will get payments from the government for every child we produce."

Hitler was a master at attracting the citizenry to his plan without revealing his true motives. People lived isolated lives in those days of limited communication. There were no radios and people travelled by foot or bicycle. They had not heard of Hitler's political book, *Mein Kampf*, which said that religion could be useful to a government, and should not be stamped out until something else had been provided to replace it. Neither had they read that in order to conquer other lands, Germany needed men ready to fight and die as well as loyal citizens to repopulate the acquired areas.

Since my father, Enne Cramer, was a leader in the community, he was asked to help organize the men so the aims of the country could reach the ears of everyone. He received books to assist him in conducting meetings properly. The country had been struggling to rebuild since the destruction brought on by World War I, and the organization of the male populace to discuss political matters would hasten the recovery.

"Give me four years in power," Hitler had shouted repeatedly, "and Germany will have advanced so much that you won't recognize the country!"

One popular promise made by this new, dynamic leader was that under his plan there would be no unemployment. Any farmer who needed help could apply to the government for a hired man. Men who could not find a job in industry would be allocated to the farmers who had applied for helpers. The farmer would furnish room and board, but the government would pay a monthly wage to each laborer.

My father applied for a farm worker, and over the years, he had three different men assisting him. Two of them were good workers, but the third was not interested in farming.

At this time citizens were asked to conduct business

with other Germans rather than with Jewish people.

"The Jews in our country claim to be Germans, but actually they are not," said Hitler. "Their first loyalty is to their Jewish traditions which prevents them from being true Germans." Initially this suggestion to patronize German businesses rather than Jewish ones did not seem to be particularly offensive.

Our First Home. The front of the building was our living quarters. The back part with the thatched roof was the attached barn. We used the attic for storage. My parents, Enne and Rike Cramer, are holding Mathilde, two, and me, Heini, nearly one. Early 1924.

We lived in a two-room house until I was seven years old. It was located in the hamlet of Juebberde in northern Germany. In addition to the two larger rooms, there were two tiny rooms the size of walk-in closets. In each of the closets was a bed that fit so tightly there was no space around it.

After we undressed in the larger room, we opened the closet door and climbed into the bed which was a large, shallow box constructed two and a half feet above the floor. The box was about eight inches deep and filled with straw. This straw was much longer than that which goes through modern machinery, for my parents cut the grain by hand, piled it in shocks, and later threshed it with a flail. A blanket over the straw completed the mattress.

Five of us children were born in this house. My baby brother, Bernhard, slept in a crib, but until the time we moved, we four older ones slept in one bed. My sisters, Mathilde, two years older than I, and Henni, two years younger, slept at the head of the bed. My small sister, Therese, and I slept at the foot. Our feet crossed in the middle, and as you might imagine, it often took a little time before we agreed on the boundaries of our foot-space and quieted enough to go to sleep.

My parents had bought the tiny farm of about seven and a half acres (three hector) before their wedding in 1920. Each of them had received a Holstein cow from their parents as a wedding gift, each had a bicycle, and they owned a wheelbarrow. Such was the extent of the worldly goods of the newlyweds. At first, my father traded work with a neighbor for the use of a horse. After a year or two, Dad bought harnesses for the cows and used them to do the farm work. He noticed, however, that when he worked them in the field, they gave less milk. The third year, he bought a horse, as one horse was sufficient to do the work on the tiny farm.

As the family grew, they considered building a larger house. However, in 1931 when I was seven years old, they found a place in Augustfehn which was about three kilometers from our original home. The house was more spacious, and there was about twice as much farmland.

When it was time to move, our neighbors, as was the custom, didn't help us. To offer assistance or to be seen watching the moving process could be construed to mean they were happy to see us go. Rather, our relatives and new neighbors came with teams and wagons to transport our belongings and to welcome us into the community. My dad's cousin, Bernhard Cramer, led a cow and I walked behind them. After a few days, our former neighbors came to visit us and to see our new farm.

We were excited about our improved location. We lived near a canal where there was a rich supply of peat moss. Also, school was closer. We could walk to school in five minutes when formerly it had taken us a half hour. The government payments for the children in our family arrived shortly after our move, and with that money, my parents bought beds with factory-made mattresses.

We had school from seven o'clock until noon in the summer, and from eight until one in the winter. Of course, with such short school days, we were assigned plenty of homework. While school subjects were not especially difficult for me, I didn't enjoy school. My thoughts were with my dad and what he might be doing on the farm.

Potatoes were our main food, and we ate them three times a day. My sisters peeled a three-gallon bucket of them every day. We ate boiled potatoes at the noon meal, and the rest of them were fried for supper and breakfast. My mother sometimes set a large skillet of fried potatoes on the table and gave each person a fork. We all ate directly from the skillet. Since our family had a large garden, we had plenty of home-grown vegetables.

On occasions, especially on Sundays, there might be something else on the table such as small servings of meat and a dessert which often was pudding topped with home-made fruit juice. Since physical labor quickly burned the calories provided by a diet that consisted mainly of vegetables, we had a lunch of tea and bread in mid forenoon and again in mid afternoon.

As you can imagine, planting our large potato patch in the spring was a major undertaking. After Dad plowed a couple rounds, we boys followed with a bucket of cut potatoes and stuck them, one by one, into the side of the furrow. When Dad made the next round, the potatoes were covered by the turning of the new furrow. A row of potatoes was planted in every second round of the plow.

I loved the farm and enjoyed the physical work that was connected with it. I hurried with my homework so that I could go outside and work with Dad. To me, hard work was a challenge which stirred my soul. I planned from early childhood to be a farmer when I grew up.

As soon as I was old enough to handle the tools used to cut peat moss, I helped my dad harvest it in spite of the fact that it was demanding physical labor. The layer of peat moss went to a depth of about eight feet along the canal. The mere fact that it was there was a defiance to me. When it was time to dig, I rejoiced at doing the work.

Heini, age 13, grade 8. Early 1937.

The top of the peat moss was lighter and easier to cut. The under layers were darker, heavier, and more valuable. We liked to get the top layers off so we could get down to the most profitable layers. It looked like gold to me because my dad either sold it for fuel or traded it for the things we needed. After it was removed from the pit, the chunks were laid in the field in neat rows to dry. A couple weeks later, we piled it and put new slabs out in the field. The piles had to be restacked periodically in order to allow the remaining moisture to evaporate. It took most of the summer to dry the peat moss.

When Mathilde was about ten and I was eight, my dad traded peat moss to a cabinet maker for some chairs and a larger table. Until that time, we children had stood around the table to eat. Now we were able to sit down for our meals, and everyone had space to have his own plate on the table. How elegant, blessed, and grown up we felt! Is it any wonder that I loved to cut peat moss?

I first became aware that we were asked to avoid doing business with the Jews when I was about eleven years old. There weren't any Jews in our hamlet, which meant we weren't well acquainted with any of them. Initially, I didn't know they were of a different nationality. I thought of them as business people because if anyone had a cow or pig to sell, they might contact a Jew who would then come to deal for it. In fact, when I was very small, someone asked me what I wanted to be when I grew up. I thought of the Jews who travelled around and executed business deals. I decided such a life would be interesting, and I answered, "I want to be a Jew."

By the year 1934, we were being told in school that it was wrong to associate with Jews. At first, my parents didn't pay much attention. They transacted business with whomever they chose. A couple years later, however, the government began applying so much pressure that my parents decided that it would be best to avoid doing business with the Jews. After all, since there were none in our village, it would be relatively easy to comply.

As was usual in the spring, my dad had a cow for sale since he had raised a replacement heifer the year before. A German man asked Dad what he wanted for the cow. The price Dad named was quite high, but finally the man agreed to it. He and Dad shook hands, which in those days cemented a deal. The man wasn't ready for the animal immediately but said he'd come for it in a couple of weeks.

Dad was in the field spreading manure when the man came back, bringing a companion with him. The two men looked at the cow and began criticizing her. Obviously they were dissatisfied with the price. Since I was small for my age, they thought I was young and wouldn't understand what they were saying. However, they misjudged me. I slipped away and ran to the field to tell Dad that, since cattle prices had gone down, the man sounded as if he wanted to back out of the deal. Dad hurried home.

The man did back out, and my dad was upset. A deal was a deal, and a man was honor-bound to consider a handshake a binding contract.

"The next person who comes and offers to buy this cow can have her," said Dad. "I don't care who he is!"

Within a few days, four Jews from another town came and bought the cow. My mother, always a hospitable woman, invited them in for tea. During tea, one of them gave each of my two small brothers a nickel. No one in our family attached any importance to these acts.

After a few days, word of the transaction reached the ears of Mr. Schuette who taught the four lower grades in our school. He was a fanatical Nazi. Since I was in the eighth grade, I sat near the door in the back of the upper-grade room. Often I could hear what was being said in the other room.

On this particular day, the lower grades had been dismissed for recess a few minutes before we were. As we were filing outside to play, we noticed some of the children in that room were clustered around the teacher's desk and that Mr. Schuette was ridiculing my young brother, Bernhard, who was a first grader.

"You should be ashamed of yourself for accepting money from a Jew," scolded the teacher. "And also, your father should be ashamed for selling a cow to a Jew."

Normally, teachers were highly respected people, but to hear this teacher ridiculing a six-year-old for the actions of a parent, was more than I could handle. Since it was recess, I reached in, grabbed my brother by the collar, and said, "C'mon, Bernhard, let's go play."

I dragged him out the door. Mr. Paul Haase, the teacher from the upper room, was in charge of the playground that day, and all went well. I was angry, though, and hurried home after school to tell my dad what had happened.

Dad decided not to ignore the incident. The next day he approached the teacher who then denied scolding my brother. Later when recess time came, Mr Schuette called to me. The playground was noisy enough so that I didn't hear his first call. He came storming down the steps, grabbed me, hit me repeatedly, and hurled me to the ground so violently that my knee was skinned.

A skinned knee was a common childhood injury. If I had received a bloody knee because I had misbehaved in school, you may be sure that I'd have gotten a second bloody knee when I got home, for my parents demanded that we behave in school. But this situation was different. My dad went back to confront the teacher, an action that caused quite a commotion.

Until this time, my father had been supportive of the Nazi party. However, this incident changed everything. He received a postcard from the local Nazi organization telling him to appear in court on a certain day. His crime was stated: he had conducted business with a Jew.

My father wrote a postcard back. "I resign from the Nazi party," he stated. "You may come to pick up the books any time you choose."

This was a difficult time for me. I felt guilty that my actions had caused so much friction. However, in looking back, it was a good thing. My father got out of the Nazi party while it was still possible to do so. Otherwise, he probably would have been dragged in deeper and deeper until, once the war started, he would have been unable to break free.

I can't recall that I ever again saw a Jew in Germany. I must admit that I didn't think about it one way or the other. I never heard a word about them being collected and sent away. If my parents suspected that something had happened to them, they didn't say anything.

Some people in our neighborhood were staunch Nazis. My parents were very careful about what they said because a remark might somehow reach their ears. It was best to make no political comments at all, not even within a family.

I graduated from the eighth grade that spring (1937). The first year after school, I helped my dad. Then Mathilde, who had been in the work force two years, returned home to assist Dad, and I got a job with a farmer, Rolf Grebner. He lived about a two-hour bike ride away from our home. I began work at Easter time, a few months before I was sixteen years old.

In September of that year Germany invaded Poland, an action which marked the beginning of World War II. I recall commenting to my boss: "If this war lasts as long as World War I did, I will probably be drafted." I worked there until February, 1941.

In the meantime, I progressed from the Hitler Youth group, which had met on Saturday forenoons, to the Advanced Hitler Youth Organization. Our required training sessions were scheduled for Wednesday evening and Sunday morning. We were never forbidden to go to church, but since our two weekly training sessions coincided exactly with the times for religious services, it was impossible for us to attend church activities.

I was assigned to a motorcycle group. Think how exciting that was for a teenager who had never ridden in a car or on any other motorized conveyance. A part of our training involved using a map to follow a trail. Two cyclists were sent down a path in opposite directions to see which would be the first to find a designated place. I loved every minute of it.

There were now seven of us children. In addition to the five who had been born in our first house, two more boys had arrived: Erich, 1933, and Enno, 1936.

2
Life in Germany

My most memorable Christmas was in 1932 when Bernhard was two years old and I was nine. On Christmas Eve, we were confined to the kitchen until chores had been completed, supper eaten, and dishes washed and put away. When all were ready to celebrate the holiday, the door between the kitchen and living room was opened, revealing the tree with the gifts underneath.

We children each received some cookies and a pair of socks or gloves, some of which had been sewn or knitted by our mother. What made this Christmas so special was that my brother, Bernhard, got a toy. It was a small wooden horse attached to a flat board with wheels underneath. The mane and tail of the tiny animal were made of real horsehair. It could be pulled across the floor by a string which was tied to the front.

All evening long, Bernhard pulled the toy, running from the living room to the kitchen, circling the table, and running back to the living room. It was the most outstanding Christmas we older kids had, seeing our little brother's excitement over that horse. He was the only one to receive a toy, but I'm sure none of the rest of us thought it unfair. No one had expected a toy, and the fact that our parents were able to afford one for the youngest in the family was a great wonder to us all.

Later, I found out that my parents had received a check for milk on the twenty-second of December. It was less than four dollars, and they owed someone two dollars. After paying the debt, they had a little money left for Christmas. Mother got sugar and spices to make cookies and they bought the toy for Bernhard.

Children began working in the field with their parents at an early age. If they were too young and clumsy to handle a hoe, they pulled weeds. At noon our parents took a short nap and we kids played along the canal. I recall that sometimes we pretended to be sailing across the ocean to America, the fantasy land where, it was said, we had a relative named Uncle Henry Bless.

When our parents arose, we all went back to the field. We came home about five o'clock, did the chores. and had supper. Then Dad was likely to read the paper while Mom went outside and tended her flowers.

The Enne Cramer Family, about 1946. Standing: Henni, Heinrich, Mathilde, Bernhard, Therese. Center: Mother Rike, Father Enne. On floor: Enno and Erich.

In the summer children went barefoot. When the weather got cold, we had to wear our clumsy wooden shoes. After lightly bouncing around on bare feet all summer, shoes made our feet feel like they were made of lead. As we walked or ran, our shoes were apt to strike the opposite ankle. The first whack wasn't so bad, but after repeated whacks, our ankles were rubbed raw. Of course, we also might get blisters on our feet, but it was the bruised, skinned ankles that gave us the most trouble.

By the time we got used to the shoes, winter was half over. A few months later, spring arrived, and we tossed our shoes aside. Our feet were soft and we often stubbed our toes. We didn't have sandburs and cockleburs in Germany, but we had plenty of thistles that had to be avoided.

Boys wore short pants even in the winter. During the colder months of the year, we wore long, wool, itchy, hand-knitted socks. Garter belts, worn around our waists, held up our socks,

We got our first suits with long pants and neckties when we were confirmed, an event that took place after we graduated from the eighth grade. What a wonderful occasion it was when we began wearing long pants! Later in life, farmers were apt to joke that the first mistake they made was taking off their neckties on Confirmation Day. They should have left them on so that they could have become bankers, lawyers, or doctors.

I don't know when bicycles came into use in Germany, but Grandma Cramer never learned to ride one. If she were to visit us, Grandpa had to harness the horse and hook up the buggy. We saw more of Grandpa than we did Grandma because he could ride a bike.

Whenever he came, he took down a four-foot tobacco pipe which hung on the wall. It was so long that when in use by a seated man, the lower end rested on the floor between his feet. The very lowest part was a fancy filigreed foot-like piece. The white porcelain bowl that held the tobacco was in the middle, perhaps two feet from the floor. The long stem was flexible.

Both Grandpa and Dad used small paper torches to light their pipes. We children cut rectangles about six or eight inches long, and folded them lengthwise five or six times. To use, one end of a strip was inserted into the front of the cooking stove to be ignited. Once a pipe was lit, the flame on the end of the torch was pinched out.

We didn't have birthday parties, but I joined the

Hitler Youth Group when I was twelve. Since school was a six-day event, youth group activities were like a holiday, for we were allowed to skip Saturday morning school in order to attend the youth meetings. Hitler was a strong believer in physical development, and much of the time at our meetings was spent in sports activities.

Grandpa Bless had passed away when I was two years old, but Grandma Bless visited us occasionally. She pedaled over on her bicycle.

I was Grandma's eldest grandson, and even though she was quite a firm person, she was more apt to listen to me than to her other grandchildren. I recall a time after the war when a few people were beginning to get family cars. My cousin, Helga Bless Onken, married a man who had a book and stationery shop. They got a car before our other relatives did. One day Grandma said to me:

"Helga offered to come in their car. She wants to drive me around the neighborhood so I can tell her how things were when I was young. What do you think of that idea?"

"Why, Grandma!" I exclaimed. "I think that would be a wonderful thing!"

"Rah!" she exclaimed. "You're just like the rest of them. Do you think at my age I'll risk my life and end up wrapped around a telephone pole?" A car was too dangerous for her, even when recommended by her eldest grandson.

Another grandson, Heini Johnson, made a small raft. Grandma sometimes climbed down the steep side of the canal, got on the raft, and paddled down the stream to a place near her friend's house. Then she climbed the slippery side of the canal after which she walked to visit her friend. That mode of travel was not too dangerous! Some years later she was persuaded to ride in a car.

I was thirteen when I got my first bicycle. My father thought I had earned it because I had helped him dig peat moss every afternoon. Since he couldn't find a second-hand bike, I became the owner of a new bike. What a proud day for me! I was jubilant. Before that time I hadn't even had a horse to ride.

Sometimes I rode my bicycle to the Dutch border. Once when I made it in two hours, my mother scolded me. It was obvious that I was riding too fast, she insisted.

"You'll have a wreck and kill yourself!" she prophesied.

In the fall of 1937, I had an afternoon job of picking up potatoes. (We went to school in the forenoons.) I earned one mark each afternoon, for a total of thirty-seven mark. In those days it was a lot of money for a kid. I had a number of ideas about how I would spend it.

During the following winter, my parents decided it was time to do something about my constant sore throat. Dad took me to another town to a specialist. I told Dad I would pay the medical costs. The doctor found I had bad tonsils, and after receiving permission, he immediately removed them.

He then told us I should spend the night in the hospital. Not wanting to stay, I begged to go home with my dad. We had ridden our bikes to the depot and had come to the town on the train. Finally, the doctor said I could go if we rented a car to take us from the depot home, and he dismissed me.

On the train, I asked my dad how much the doctor had charged, but he didn't tell me. When we got to Augustfehn, I felt sure I could ride my bike, and we pedalled home.

Later I learned that the doctor had charged twenty mark. I was a rather quiet boy, and I had been taught to respect other people, especially teachers, policemen, doctors, and the like. But the amount of the bill made me furious. Twenty mark for a half hour's work? I had spent twenty afternoons of back-breaking work earning that amount. I was deeply disappointed.

I began learning to spin yarn in 1939 when I was sixteen years old. I was working as a hired hand for a family who had three sons. This family had a hired girl, and she began keeping company with the middle son who was in the military. The lady of the house told her that since she was going with her son, she expected her to learn how to spin. The girl practiced during the long winter evenings. Sometimes when she got up from the spinning wheel, I sat down and spun. My grandmother Bless had a spinning wheel, and when I quit work at the farm, she loaned it to me.

Grandma had a hostess chair in the kitchen near the window. She loved to serve tea. One time I was spading her lawn in front of the window. They had decided that year to plant potatoes there. Every hour or so she knocked on the window and held up her cup which was the signal that it was time for tea. My goal was to get the spading done, but it was an honor to drink tea with Grandma. I laid down the shovel and went inside.

I have happy memories of Grandma Bless. From the time I got my bike and began going to visit her until I left for America when I was 27, she always shook my hand when it was time for me to go home. "Come back soon," she would say. "I won't live very long."

Once when Mathilde was knitting, my two younger sisters were peeling potatoes. For some reason, they were sitting on the edge of the kitchen table as they peeled. Henni slid off the table, and as she fell to the floor, the knife pierced through the palm of her left hand. When she pulled it out, blood began to spurt.

Dad and I were working in the barn which was attached to the house. One of the kids came running to get help.

Dad wrapped Henni's hand tightly and with her riding on the front of the bike, he pedalled to town. In those days there were no doctor's appointments. The patients sat in the office and waited their turns. However, in letting a patient out of the office door, the doctor saw Henni. He said to Dad, "I can see there is an emergency. You come next."

After the doctor repaired the wound, Henni stayed with Aunt Gretchen Cramer who was a registered nurse. She bathed the wound daily and kept it carefully wrapped. The main artery in her hand had been injured, and after a week or two it broke open and began to spurt blood again. Using her bicycle, Aunt Gretchen again took her to the doctor. Eventually the wound healed, but the index finger was stiff and crooked.

One day I was visiting my great-uncle, Meko Cramer, and he inquired about Henni's hand.

I explained about the stiff, crooked index finger. "The doctor says it is useless and in the way. He is going to amputate it."

Uncle Meko looked thoughtful and spoke slowly. "No-o-o-o," he said. "No-o-o, he won't."

I was surprised by his objection. Why would he try to overrule the doctor's judgment?

"I will go immediately and talk to your dad," he said. He rode my bike and I walked.

"That finger can be removed any time," he told Dad. "But once it is off, it can never be replaced. I suggest that you wait with the amputation and try to regenerate the finger. Each evening, bend it back and forth as much as you can. Then tape it to a stick overnight. Each night make the tension a bit tighter in an effort to straighten it. If it doesn't work, you can then have it amputated."

Dad followed his advice which was a good thing. The finger was returned to normal use.

When I began working for Rolf Grebner, my parents told my boss that they expected me to be in bed by nine o'clock. There was no question. At nine o'clock I went to a little hallway where I slept and went to bed. At six in the morning, my boss walked by and gave one little tap on the door. I got up and followed him to the barn where we milked about 20 cows.

I have no idea what would have happened if I hadn't responded to that first gentle call. I never tried staying in bed for a minute or two more. My hours had been agreed upon, and it did not occur to me to test the limits.

Wooden yokes that rested across our shoulders were used to carry the milk. A chain dangled from each end of the yoke, and a bucket of milk was hooked to each chain. When a person first began to use a yoke, it was awkward, and the milk was apt to splash. However, it wasn't long before one learned to walk without spilling a single drop.

Another handy device that we had in Germany was a container for sowing grain by hand. It was made of galvanized tin and shaped to fit a person's waist. There was a strap that went over the shoulder. It was the right height for a person to reach in and get a handful of seed grain.

Sometimes we have seen pastors giving sermons about sowing grain, and as they talk they might illustrate what they are saying by flinging their arm out in a sowing motion. Invariably, they do it backwards. If the worker takes a handful of grain and sows as he flings his arm away from his body, he is sowing through the crack of his half-opened hand, which means that the grains will fall in a thick, narrow band. The correct way is for him to take a handful of grain, swing his closed hand back, loosen his grip a little as he brings it forward, and let the grain slide out between his fingers. This motion effectively separates the grains and spreads them more evenly. With a little practice, the motion becomes rhythmic. As the sower puts his left foot forward, he grabs a handful of seed, and as he puts his right foot forward, he spreads.

In the winter cows were tied in rows in the barn. Behind them was a gutter to catch the manure. Night and morning the gutters were cleaned and the manure hauled out with a wheelbarrow. In the summer we were busy with planting, hoeing, and harvesting. All the work was done by hand, of course.

3
Into Battle

In the two and a half years between the onset of the war and the end of 1941, Hitler's blitz attacks on surrounding countries had brought more than a dozen nations under the Nazi flag. Also, he was conducting an on-going attack on England who was protected from the fearsome Nazi tanks by the English Channel.

On June 22, 1941, Hitler attacked Russia which was ruled by the Communist dictator, Joseph Stalin. Nazi troops advanced at an astonishing pace, arriving within 200 miles of Moscow after a few weeks of fighting. But the Communists managed to regroup and prepare a resistance. Then severe winter weather became Stalin's ally, and his troops were able to hold the Nazis back.

The United States had entered the war at the end of 1941 when Japan, who had a pact with Germany, bombed Pearl Harbor.

In February, 1942, I was called for a preinduction physical examination. I welcomed the invitation because all my friends were going into military service. I was disappointed when I didn't pass the physical. In order to enter the army, one had to weigh at least a hundred pounds, and at age seventeen, I weighed less than ninety. However, I began to grow about that time, and by June I was heavy enough to enter.

I had my boot training in Bremen. Since I loved horses, I wanted to be in the cavalry, but my request was denied. I was placed in the anti-aircraft unit which also helped protect the infantry. We had small cannons which used twenty millimeter bullets. Most of the time, the cannons were mounted on a half-track, a vehicle similar to a small Caterpillar and about the size of a three-quarter ton pickup. We could fold down the sides of the box so the cannon could be turned in a 360 degree circle.

Heinrich Cramer, Soldier. 1942.

First we had general boot training. Two weeks after we had begun it, I was chosen to be a Morse coder. Most of the fellows in that unit were from a college because they had formerly been deferred to finish the semester. It was at a time when the semester had ended, and they were drafted into the service.

Since I had quit school after the eighth grade, I was at a decided disadvantage. I knew if I were to keep up, I would have to spend considerable time studying. I made a surprising discovery: If I studied, I could learn. Until this time, studying had been a bore. Now I was encouraged and worked diligently. We were tested daily and were ranked according to our scores. I never did make the top score, but I got up to the second highest.

I would like to make a remark here to anyone who works with young children or youths. It is extremely important to encourage them. When I was in school, my teacher always told me, "I know you can do it." At the time, my grades weren't too good, and I wasn't sure he was right. However, as I studied Morse Coding, those words came back to me. I found out his assessment was correct. In subsequent years, those were words that I lived by. Even today when I am faced with a difficult task, I hear my teacher's voice, "You can do it!" I then gather my wits, and I do it!

At the end of our boot training, we had a three-day mock battle in the woods. Since I was a Morse coder, I carried my coding equipment on my back. Whenever we paused in our march, I'd back up to a tree, lift myself on tiptoes, press the pack against the tree, and lower my heels to the ground. This action placed some of the weight of my equipment on the tree.

After three days, we came to a village. We hoped this was the end of the exercise, for we were footsore and exhausted. Just outside the village, we were lined up, 160 men in four groups. I was in the third group.

"I know you are tired," said our commander. "But it is important for us to enter this town and make a good impression. I want you to march as a proud soldier!" He stepped to the side.

A band made up of bass horns and drums was in front of us. It struck up a rousing tune and led the way. Our tired legs seemed to move automatically with the music. The commander stood on the street corner. During the entire six weeks of our basic training, I had never once seen him smile, but now he grinned and saluted us. It was quite an experience.

We stayed in a schoolhouse for a couple of days after which we went back to our original training grounds. From there we were sent home on furlough. We were told that after our furloughs, we could expect to be sent into battle on the front line.

One of my friends, Fritz Schoene, was in boot camp with me. We stayed together as much of the time as possible. After we got home, he told his family that he would be sent into the front line. The last Sunday that he was home, his relatives congregated at his house to wish him well. I didn't have the heart to tell my family. I didn't want to worry them. My visit home was quiet, ordinary, and with no difficult farewells. Our furlough ended on a Wednesday. He was sent into France, and I was routed toward the Front in the Russian sector.

Our company with the necessary supplies made up a small train with forty men travelling in each boxcar We were enroute fourteen days and fifteen nights. The reason it took so long was that provisions to the Front were shipped by rail and since they had priority, we were often sidetracked to make way for the supply trains. Our small stove in the middle of each boxcar did little to warm the space, for the Russian November air was frigid. We were cold and bored.

We rejoiced when we finally reached our destination since those two weeks on the train were not pleasant. We found out after arriving, however, that the slowness of our journey was a lifesaver. Had we arrived a day and a half sooner, we would have been sent as replacements to Stalingrad. As anyone who knows much about World War II can tell you, not many German soldiers survived the lengthy, fierce battle of Stalingrad.

The Russian front was divided into three sections. When we got off the train, twenty-five of us were assigned duty in the middle section. Getting there required a two-day walk. During that forty-eight hour period, we saw enough of war to last a lifetime, and we hadn't yet experienced battle.

A few days before, there had been a Russian breakthrough. The Germans had regained the lost ground, but now as we passed through, we were confronted with the awful signs of warfare. I remember one incident vividly.

As we passed through a woods, we could smell the enticing odor of roast meat. Here in the woods, that roast smelled wonderful, but I couldn't figure out where the odor was originating. Then we came upon an exploded tank that had burned. Engulfed in sudden horror, I realized that what I smelled was the odor of burned bodies. The men had been baked inside the tank.

When we arrived at the front, I was not immediately put into battle. I was eighteen, but I was of slight build, and I hadn't yet begun to shave. I suppose I looked like a kid to the commander. I became his attendant, though since I was a Morse coder, I sometimes did work at coding or decoding messages. Each day the code was changed, which meant that keeping up with the day's code was an added requirement.

When the code was changed, the new code was taken to the various points on the front line where a coder was situated. Each day a coder was required to document that he had destroyed the old code and had received the new one. Sometimes in the heat of battle, it was necessary to flee. The coder must, if at all possible, grab the heavy pack of coding supplies as he ran. In the event that a code pack was lost, the coder had a difficult time explaining. Luckily, I never abandoned or lost my coding supplies.

Eventually, I was put into the front line as a coder. It was a harrowing experience. I have a medal at home called a Storm Medal. It is given to men who have three times been close enough to the enemy to see the whites of their eyes. To be face-to-face with an armed enemy is a horrible experience. To those who are reading this story, I'm sure you can imagine that something terrible must happen in such a situation. Since I am here, you can figure it out. You probably would like to know the details of these encounters, but I can't tell you. Even after all this time, I can't talk about it. There is no glory in war.

The Storm Medal is the only one I received. I was wounded near the end of the war, but I didn't get the German equivalent of the Purple Heart. By that time, the country was in confusion, and when the war ended, the Allies took over. No German medals were given after that.

This is a good place to say that I love thunderstorms. I will love them for as long as I live, and with good reason. Whenever it began to lightning on the battlefield, it was a true blessing because the fighting stopped. Both sides ceased firing because the lightning could be drawn to our cannons and guns. The violence of the storm, the wind, the flashing lightning, and the crashing thunder, filled the air, but it was quiet in comparison to the deafening noises of battle.

During a rain, there were times when we lifted our heads and waved to the Russians. Often they waved back. What a godsend to be free from war for a little while. Nowadays some people think an electrical storm is a danger, but to me it will always signify safety.

I don't care to tell the details of that first year in battle. With so much killing, it is a surprise that I lived through it, surviving one day after the next, on and on, when it seemed that surely it was my turn to go next. We advanced to a point west of Moscow before we slowly began, hill by hill and town by town, to give ground back to the Communists. The problem was that with the threat of a second front in western Europe, we were not receiving the supplies we needed to maintain the vast eastern front.

Once three other men and I were sent on an errand. For several days we were away from our company. Bursting shells were crashing down in our area with such regularity that finally we hardly noticed them, but we were exhausted and sick of the sights and sounds and smells of battle. We wished that just for awhile we could lie down and have a few hours of uninterrupted sleep.

We came to a part of an old barn. Since it was evening, we went inside and lay down to rest. The shells continued to rain around us.

I thought, "Lord, I've had enough. I have no desire to keep living. Let this barn explode while we sleep so that I won't have to go through any more of this madness. Comfort my mother, and somehow let her know that I died at peace in the midst of all this lunacy." I felt calm and went to sleep thinking that one of the many descending shells would surely blast us away, bringing an end to the insane existence. I have no idea what the other fellows were thinking because we didn't reveal our thoughts to each other. I slept all night and was surprised to be alive the next morning. Shells were still exploding, but somehow they continued to miss us. We returned to our outfit, all of us alive for the moment.

I recall an incident when I was on guard duty. A small group of us had arrived in a certain area and didn't know yet what the situation was. We were quite a distance from our headquarters. There was a small village several kilometers away, and for some reason we were ordered to have a guard on duty there.

It was a miserably cold night. The wind was blowing snow on the ground and sleet in the air. My time was from two until four o'clock in the morning, and because of the distance, I was taken there by vehicle. After my buddy left and I was in position, I felt uneasy. The snow skittered across the ground, rolling in ghostly sheets when the wind gusted. I had a feeling that someone was sneaking up on me, gliding from one hut to the next. It seemed when there was a sudden blast of wind, there were more noises than just the rolling snow.

I shivered with both cold and fear. In spite of the fact that I sensed danger, there was nothing to do but stay in position and be as watchful as possible. I tried to exercise my stiff fingers in the event I needed to use my gun.

Then a vehicle came swooping up and my buddy leaped out.

"It's time to get out of here!" he said. He brought an order for me to return to headquarters. I was glad to go!

The enemy liked to capture someone from an outpost in the hope of gaining information from him. I think if I had stayed, I'd have gotten a gunny sack over my head and would have been spirited away. The next day we moved on.

As the months and years of the war piled up, gasoline became scarce. We captured some of the Russian ponies and began using them to haul food to the front lines. Since I loved working with horses, I pined for the job. I asked to be transferred, but my request was denied because I was too valuable as a Morse coder.

Time passed while I watched other men handle the horses. Then an idea entered my head. What if I no longer was valuable as a Morse Coder? What if I forgot how?

One morning I awoke and reported that I couldn't recall a single thing about Morse coding! My mind was a total blank. Five days went by, and I still insisted I couldn't remember. Since I was worthless as a coder, someone finally asked the question I was waiting to hear. "Do you think you can handle a team of horses?"

"I guess so," I said. "Anyway I'll give it a try."

I began hauling food to the front line, using a four-horse team of small Welsh ponies. For the first time in my army career, I had a job I liked. Soup for 160 men was cooked in a huge cast iron kettle which we called a "goulash cannon". The soup was transferred into milk cans and set in the wagon. Also, there were cheeses, black bread, and occasionally lunch meat. Sometimes meals could be delivered in the daytime, but not always. If we had to go over hills where we could be seen by the enemy, we were forced to deliver during darkness.

I wasn't satisfied with the fact that I drove four fine horses. I wanted a pony for myself. When I went past the German Headquarters of another company, I noticed they had quite a few horses. Probably, when their gas supply got low, they "confiscated" them from Russian civilians. I reasoned that the horses weren't theirs to begin with, and that one of them just as well be mine.

One afternoon when I passed near their headquarters, I saw a horse standing near the road. I caught it and got it through the fence, after which I tied it to the back of the wagon. I travelled on until I came to a rise where I would be exposed to the enemy if I proceeded in daylight. I stopped in a valley to wait for the cover of darkness. There was a bunker nearby which was in the hands of our company. I went inside.

Presently, one of my buddies came in and told me that someone outside wanted to see me. We went out. A fellow from the other company had followed me and obviously knew I had taken a horse. He stuck out his chin and looked at me with an expression that let me know I had better deliver some acceptable answers.

"You stole one of our ponies!" he said, glaring at me.

Like the rest of us, he spoke in High German, but I thought I detected a familiar accent. I answered in Low German, the vernacular in the northern part of Germany.

"If the horse is yours," I said, "you are welcome to have him back."

"Are you from the Bremen area?" he inquired, grinning. We were both glad to find someone who was from the same part of the country and who spoke the dialect with which we were familiar. We had a pleasant visit. The encounter could have ended in a fight, but instead I found a new friend.

My first attempt to get a horse of my own had failed, but I did not give up. Because of the concentration of troops along the front line, we were always short of supplies. I decided to use a different tactic.

Whenever we got our rations, there were always a few cigarettes included as well as a bottle of schnapps. At that time I didn't smoke, and I never did have any use for whisky. The Russians were short of vodka, and were always glad to get their hands on a bottle of any kind of alcoholic beverage, but one or two bottles were not enough to buy a horse. I began saving cigarettes which I traded to other soldiers for schnapps. After I had collected enough of the fiery liquid, I was able to trade it to a Russian for a pony.

Once I was in a wooded area on my way back to camp after making a delivery to the front. Suddenly,

Allied planes were overhead, and were shooting with machine guns down into the grove. There was an old building nearby which I felt would provide a little more cover, and whipping my horses to a run, we dashed to it. I leaped out of the wagon and keeping the lines of the horses in my hands, I threw myself to the ground on the shady side of the building. I was aware that I had landed on something, but I lay still until the planes were gone. When I arose, I found . . . that I had . . . lain on a . . . corpse. It was a German soldier. For a moment, I sat beside him and prayed for his mother. Then I did the only thing I could. On legs as numb as wooden ones, I got in my wagon and drove away to complete my orders.

The Russian civilians were truly good people. The Communists were in power, but most of the inhabitants on farms and in villages were not Communists, though they wouldn't have dared to say so. Secretly I'm sure they hoped the Communists would be driven from their land. The ordinary Russian citizens were the most generous people I have ever met. Sometimes I approached them, and always found them to be friendly, helpful, and peace-loving even though our countries were enemies. They might be short of food themselves, but they were always willing to share.

I got tired of eating from a goulash can all the time. One day when we were stationed at Rogashev near the Dnieper River, I knocked on the door of a Russian house. A woman answered the door. By that time I could speak Russian fairly well, for I've never had much trouble learning languages. I introduced myself and told her I assumed that she was short of certain food items.

"I have some sugar, flour, and salt," I told her. "Since you live on a farm, I imagine you have milk and an egg or two. Would it be all right if we pooled our food items and had pancakes together?"

She was agreeable. She invited me in, and I found that she had three young sons, ages eleven to fourteen. The pancakes were a wonderful treat. Our company was stationed nearby for about two weeks, and the Russian family and I became friends. After a few days, I asked her where her husband was. She burst into tears.

"He's been taken away," she said. "I don't know if he is dead or alive. If he lives, he's probably in Siberia. He was an ambitious man, and as a result, we had a little more than most people--probably a little more than we should have had. One night there was a commotion and a knock on the door. When my husband answered the door, the Communist police grabbed him and took him away. They also took a couple cows and a few other things. That is all I know. I haven't heard from him since."

I got disgusted with one of the four horses that I drove on the food wagon because he was balky. Even though he was a big, muscular animal, his tugs were slack most of the time. One day when I didn't have to haul supplies, I decided to do two things. I would clean the stalls and I would, for once, make that balky horse do a little work. I backed the wagon into position and pitched on the manure. Then I hitched up the horse, but I couldn't get him to move. I tried everything I could think of, but he was just as determined as I was. He wouldn't budge.

Finally I got a handful of straw and placed it under him, thinking that if I set it afire, he would take off. About that time my boss, who was a blacksmith as a civilian, came along.

"You aren't going to fire that straw, are you?" he asked.

"Yes, I am," I told him. "This horse has balked the whole time I've had him. I'm finally determined that one way or the other, he is going to do a little work.

"Then you get in the wagon and get a good hold on the lines," said the boss, "and I'll put a match to the straw." The horse merely stomped around, put out the fire, and still wouldn't go.

Later this horse was wounded, and was butchered for food. I placed my own pony in the harness, and he proved to be a willing worker.

One Sunday afternoon in June, 1944, we were

stationed in a village. Another company had been stationed there also, but they had pulled out in the forenoon. I had been hoping to find some pieces of rope to tie the ponies, and I decided to go to the grounds that had recently been vacated to see if I could find some. While I was gone, our company prepared to move out. When I got back, the boss was stomping around.

"Where have you been?" he shouted. He handed me a note. "Leave now! Deliver this message, and don't waste any time." He showed me a point on the map. "We'll meet you here Tuesday afternoon."

Except for me, the company was motorized. They pulled out immediately. I had to harness my horses, toss the things I needed into the wagon, and deliver a message, all tasks that put me behind. On Tuesday when I arrived at the appointed place, there was no sign of our company. With the demand for supplies and men on the new Western Front, the Eastern front was thinned, a situation which forced us to retreat. A steady stream of traffic filled the roads. Everyone was heading west.

I had a hard time getting into the string of vehicles. There were forty or fifty wagons in every company, and once they were arranged in single file, they wouldn't allow space for other wagons to get in the line because it would separate the company.

After much waiting and maneuvering, I finally managed to get onto the crowded road. Once I had found a place, I was careful to keep it. My main worry was that my horses needed food and water in order to function. Could I care for them well enough to preserve their strength?

I knew that if the horses gave out, my flight would be considerably more difficult. I was always looking for opportunities to give them food or water. One day I found an abandoned sack of potatoes. I put it in my wagon, and whenever I had a spare minute, I took out my pocket knife and sliced potatoes. Then I cut straw into inch or inch and a half lengths and mixed it with the potatoes. This mixture I fed to the horses.

4
Moving Westward

Several fellows who were afoot asked if they might get in my wagon. I told them they could ride on one condition. Whenever the line of traffic slowed to a stop, they must immediately jump out and pull grass for the horses. All except one complied with my wish. It didn't take long to get rid of the slacker.

My biggest problem was exhaustion, for I hadn't slept for days. Even when we were stopped by a traffic problem, I had to stay alert in order to keep the wagon in the line. Also, everyone, animal and man, was thirsty and hungry, with thirst being the worse of the two. Once we stopped by a moss-covered puddle near the roadside. While the horses drank, I brushed the moss aside, put my face down to the water, and drank in the same way they did. I thought I might get sick, but I didn't.

Because we weren't hauling a heavy load, I used two horses to pull the wagon and tied the other two behind where they could get some rest. We could feed the two at the back as we moved along. At times when the line of vehicles halted because of a traffic problem, we switched the horses. This method of rotation would, I knew, make the best use of the energy of the team.

One time we came to a place where a river bridge was out. There were hundreds of teams, motorcycles, bicycles, and pedestrians milling about, wondering how to proceed. To add to our concern, there were often Allied planes flying over. Some people were in groups and had to wait for the decisions of their leaders, but I was my own boss. I decided to look for a place where the bank was less steep and try fording the river.

At that time I had one passenger. In order to lighten the load, we threw away all the supplies we could spare. Among the articles we discarded was a pair of new pants.

I was concerned with the life-and-death struggle of crossing the river before the enemy army cut us off, and my mind was fuzzy with weariness. The new pants didn't seem of much importance even though the ones I was wearing were old and needed laundering. Later I wished I had discarded them and had put on the new pants.

As we moved along the river bank, we came to a man who was in a covered wagon pulled by a beautiful pair of Belgian horses. He coaxed the team down the steep bank, and when they lurched into the water, the man was hurled forward. The wagon tumbled atop him and the horses. In a tangle of harnesses, man and animals churned about in the deep water. We watched helplessly from the high bank, for there was no way we could help them. I presume they all drowned.

We continued on, looking for a place where the banks on either side would be more shallow. When I found a likely place, I talked to my passenger.

"You may ride if you choose," I told him, "but only as a piece of luggage. I want no static from you. No remarks. No actions that would distract either me or the horses. You saw what happened to the covered wagon. For us to avoid a similar tragedy, total concentration is demanded of both me and the team. If you want out, you get out now because I don't want to hear a sound from you once we enter the water." He decided to stay in the wagon and take the chance.

My lightweight, Welsh ponies were willing and manageable. I urged them down the bank and into the water. For a while they were able to wade, but as the riverbed fell away they were forced to swim. I was unmindful of Hitler's exhortations that religion was not necessary, and I was praying with all my heart and soul. I prayed for strength for my tired horses. I prayed that the current in the middle of the river wouldn't carry us away. I prayed, as I looked down at the water swirling around our ankles, that the wagon wouldn't sink. I prayed that the bank on the opposite side would be shallow enough to allow us to climb out.

You can be sure there were two grateful young men when the team finally struggled out of the river. Those brave little horses! We let them rest, heads down, wheezing, for ten or fifteen minutes before proceeding onward. Then keeping an eye on the skies for Allied planes, we urged our faithful ponies westward

After about four more days, we made it to Minsk where there was a train in operation. Some fellows there said they would get us passage on the train if we would sell them our horses. I gave those courageous ponies a few appreciative pats, and walked away from them.

The trains usually pushed two flat beds loaded with sand ahead of the locomotive. If there was a mine under the track, the weight of the loaded flatcars would blow it before the engine reached it. The only seat available for us was on one of the flat beds in front of the locomotive, but I was so exhausted that I wasn't choosy.

The next day we reached a company of German soldiers who were setting up a defense with the idea of holding the Communists back. We were assigned to mount a cannon behind a jeep, after which we camouflaged it. Next we dug holes for our own protection. I found some brush to put over mine.

Once that fall of 1944, while we were stationed about ten or twelve miles from Minsk, another soldier and I were given orders to go to Minsk for supplies. We had no gasoline, and no team or wagon. We decided that the only way we could carry out the order was to borrow a horse and wagon from a farm. There was a Russian house nearby. When we knocked, two couples came out the door. One couple was young and the other was elderly.

I said, "We need to borrow a team and wagon to go to Minsk. I assure you that we will return it."

The old lady was the boldest of the four. "We don't have a team and wagon," she said.

"We know you do," my buddy told her. "We saw you using it a few days ago. We need it only for today and will bring it back in the evening."

She wouldn't trust us and kept insisting they had no

horses or wagon. We looked around. Finally I saw the tip of the wagon tongue sticking out from under a pile of hay. The young man gave in, went into the woods, and brought the horses. While we were hitching them, the old lady grabbed the lines and got into the wagon.

"I'm going with you," she insisted.

I answered, "Lady, you can't go. We aren't allowed to take civilians with us."

"I'm going!" she stated emphatically.

We tried to persuade her to let go of the lines, but she wouldn't. I even took out my gun and told her I'd shoot her through the hands, but still she held on. We didn't like scuffling with her in front of her family.

My buddy and I conferred. We decided we'd take her a short way after which we would put her out of the wagon. When we got about a half kilometer from the place, my buddy signalled to me, and we grabbed her. In spite of her kicking and screaming, it was easy to overpower her and put her out of the wagon. We told her again we would return the horses and wagon and drove away, leaving her standing in the middle of the road, scolding, crying, and shaking her fist.

After completing our orders, we drove toward the farm. The young man saw us and walked out to meet us. He was carrying a small, skinny duck which he offered to us, all the while thanking us profusely for the return of the wagon. We didn't accept the duck. We turned the horses over to him, and walked back to camp.

We were stationed at that place for about three weeks. During that time, I could have asked the family for anything, and if they would have had it, they'd have given it to me. They were wonderful people.

One time when I was awakened to relieve a man on patrol, he said, "Listen to the rumbling in the distance. It must be tanks on the move."

During the two hours I was on guard, the rumble continued. When my replacement came we discussed the noise again. The air was charged with expectancy.

Dawn brought a lovely fall day. I was in my foxhole

writing a letter. I made a point of writing to someone every day, to my parents, a neighbor, a cousin, or a friend. Since confusion abounded, military messages sometimes got fouled up. If my parents received a telegram that said I had been killed on the fifth, and later someone in the neighborhood got a letter from me written on the sixth, my family would know I was still alive.

Suddenly about ten o'clock, our world exploded. The enemy must have fired every weapon they had at us. Our cannon blew up along with almost everything else in our camp. One of my buddies leaped into the foxhole with me. His face was bloody from minor wounds and dirty from the ground kicked up by the exploding shells.

I reached outside to grab my gun, but it had been demolished. The largest piece was about eighteen inches long. As soon as we were able to leave our holes, we sneaked out and fled. I left the gun behind, for it was useless and would only be in my way. Late in the afternoon I found my outfit, and I went immediately to the supply clerk for a gun.

He said, "Where is your old one?"

"It got blown up," I said.

"Can you prove it?" he asked.

My temper began to flare. "Well, you are welcome to go look at it," I said with a snort.

"As you know," he stated, "I have to have proof before I can issue another."

I was exhausted and also shaken from our near escape. I had my steel helmet in my hands. I hurled it to the ground, bouncing it in front of his toes.

"One more word and you've had it," I shouted. "I need a rifle. You can either get it for me, or I'll get it myself. If you don't want to believe my gun was destroyed, you can go where I was, and see for yourself."

He issued me a gun.

Finally we were shoved back to the border between Poland and Germany. There was a small river separating us from the Communists. Every night for three nights the Russians built a bridge across it, and every day we blew it up with our cannons.

A group of East German soldiers came past us and stopped for awhile. They had received special assignments because we were fighting near the locality where they had lived as civilians.

We agreed to cover them. After they were in position to go forward, we planned to shoot our cannons, aiming just ahead of them. When they were ready to storm the Russians, they would signal us with a flare so we would know to stop shooting. We set our watches to the second.

I don't know if it was fate or espionage, but three minutes before we were to begin the attack, the Russians stormed us. Of the company of special soldiers, only three or four came back. Oh, I was sick of war! I'd have welcomed a wound severe enough to get me out of it.

Soon afterward I was sitting with crossed legs in my foxhole behind the brush I had piled in front of it. There was intermittent shooting going on all the time, but I was numb and wasn't paying much attention to it. All at once a shell exploded nearby, and a piece of shrapnel came hissing into the foxhole. Since it was embedded in the ground near my leg, I took out my pocket knife and dug it out. It was about five inches long.

I turned it over and over in my hand, thinking that its jagged, razor-sharp edges would do considerable damage if it hit a person. A surprising thought leaped into my mind: I wished my leg had been far enough forward to be in its pathway. At that point, I'd have been glad to lose a leg to get out of the middle of the battle.

Because the Russians were advancing on both sides, we were again forced to pull back. Our company formed a line and moved westward. Once when we were held up momentarily because of the congestion on the roads, I noticed some Russians, a woman and several children, that I had previously befriended. I wondered what they could be doing, standing here on a street corner far from their homes. I handed the lines to my buddy.

"You drive," I told him. "I'll be back in a minute. I

want to talk to my friends."

I jumped out of the wagon and walked over to the Russians.

"I'm surprised to see you here," I said to them after I had greeted them. "What brings you so far?"

I found they had abandoned their homes and were fleeing from the Communists. They were Russians, but they weren't Communists. We were soon engrossed in conversation. I was dimly aware that the traffic was intermittently inching ahead, but I was sure I could catch up. However, I talked too long, and before I knew it, my entire company was gone.

I hurried down the road, looking for my buddies but couldn't find them. I came to a town which I thought was the place where we were to spend the night, but all was confusion. I met no one I recognized. Then I turned a corner and met a scene that chilled my blood. A German soldier was hanging from a tree. Above him was a sign: "I was too chicken to fight for our women and children back home. That's why I'm hanging here." Obviously, he had been considered a deserter and was a German hung by Germans.

Deep inside, I was quivering like a fish on a spear. If I were accosted by the Military Police, they would think I was a deserter, for I had no documentation to give me permission to be separated from my unit. I had faced death hundreds of times, but to be hanged in disgrace was a horror my mind couldn't accept.

I decided it would be safer for me to rely on the help of civilians rather than to approach a German. I knocked on the door of a Russian house, praying all the time that I had not chosen the home of a Communist. Even though I was from the side of the enemy, the Russians gave me supper and allowed me to stay overnight.

By morning, I had fabricated a story I hoped would be believable and also had partially calmed my nerves. With the help of directions given by my Russian benefactors, I found the headquarters of a German company. Even though my insides were like jelly, I managed to approach with a semblance of bravado.

"I'm looking for my company headquarters," I told the officer in charge. "We had a terrible battle and were almost wiped out. I've been sent to ask for more supplies and reinforcements, but I can't find our headquarters. Do you know where they are?" Most of what I said was true, but actually, my company had not been involved in the particular battle that I mentioned.

He looked at me intently, and began asking questions to see if I were telling the truth. Because I had recently worked at Morse coding and also at delivering supplies, I knew much more about the positions, problems, and activities of the various companies than did most soldiers. I must have been convincing, for he told me the way to my company's headquarters.

"I have one more request," I said. "I haven't any written orders. In the confusion of the battle I was hurriedly sent on my way, and not given a written pass. Could you write me a pass that would protect me until I reach our headquarters?" I told him about the German soldier I had seen hanging from a tree. All the while, I was praying earnestly that he would believe me.

Again he eyed me suspiciously and asked more questions. I answered any way I could, truthfully or otherwise, in order to be convincing. I pride myself in being an honest person, but when my life was at stake, I found I could be quite a believable liar. Finally, he wrote a pass for me.

Since we got no news reports, we could only guess about conditions on the Western Front. Rumors said, however, that the Western Allies were advancing. To us on the Eastern Front, it was obvious there was a limit to the ground we could lose and still keep fighting. By this time we had been pushed back into Poland. Was the fighting nearly over? If so, we hoped to surrender to the British or Americans rather than to the Communists.

One day three other fellows and I were traveling on a half-track. A shell exploded in the air, and shrapnel rained down on us. I didn't realize I had been hit, but I could see the others were wounded. The driver immediately drove us to an emergency center.

The doctor was doing surgery on a man who had lost a leg. He needed to roll the patient over, and I had arrived in time to assist him. Next I began helping one of my buddies cut his pant leg open so we could tend to his wound. Gradually, I became aware that my right foot was wet, and was getting more and more soggy as the minutes went by.

Upon examination, I discovered I had a flesh wound in my right leg. Also I had a couple pieces of shrapnel in my left shoulder blade. Those pieces were never removed which means I have carried some Russian metal in me for more than half a century. I claim that having iron parts in my body has made me tougher.

Since my buddies were more seriously wounded than I was, I continued on by myself. I was hoping I could get near enough to the American Army so I could surrender to them rather than to the Communists who either executed prisoners or condemned them to a slow death in frigid Siberia. I daydreamed that I would be sent to America as a prisoner of war, and could then contact Henry Bless, the uncle for whom I was named. He was an American citizen living near Madison, Nebraska.

Finally I reached Gdansk, a Polish city on the Baltic Sea. Upon inquiring, I found a German military headquarters. I told them who I was and why I was traveling alone. This time I was able to tell the truth, but I divulged only enough to serve my purpose.

They had eight Russian prisoners which they were anxious to transport. They put me in charge of them and sent us to another place by train. At the depot I considered the confusion, the near-end of the war, and the need for men to return to civilian life. Before time to board the train, I told the Russians that I had no reason to detain them and gave them permission to go where they chose. I hope they managed to get to their homes.

I recall a sad event when we were in Poland. We were in a little dugout in no-man's-land which was within sight of a Polish cabin. I don't know if it was Russian artillery or ours, but someone shot into the house, and it began to burn. The civilian owner struggled with water buckets and extinguished the fire. A victory! However, the next morning the house, again caught in the cross-fire, burst into flames a second time. The man reappeared and risked his life to fight the blaze. He struggled doggedly, but this time the cabin burned to the ground. I wished I could have helped him. Probably most of what he owned had gone up in smoke.

Suddenly, the Communist Army became more aggressive because they were in a hurry to get to Berlin before the Americans arrived there. They pushed us aside onto a long, narrow peninsula that extends into the Bay of Danzig. It forms a part of the Polish Corridor, and is perhaps three kilometers wide and thirty-five or forty kilometers long. Once we were on the peninsula, the Russians had a simple way to keep us prisoners. They occupied the base of the peninsula and left us to care for ourselves any way we could.

In addition to being inhabited by a multitude of soldiers, the peninsula was crowded with hundreds of horses and wagons. They had been abandoned earlier by refugees who arrived on the peninsula while there were ships using the harbor. Those refugees had been removed by the ships. Had it not been that we were considered prisoners of the enemy, the situation would have been quite pleasing to me, for there were horses of every age, breed, size, and color. Prisoner or not, I decided to enjoy myself as long as I could.

Each day I caught a different team of horses, chose a wagon or carriage, and drove around the peninsula, offering grand rides to anyone who was interested. Some people chided me for wasting my energy, and some thought I was foolish for amusing myself when the situation was grim. However, I told them that enjoying the animals on the peninsula made our predicament not one iota worse. There was plenty of time to bewail our fate if we were executed or sent to Siberia.

5
On the Ship

When I talked to the horses, I reverted to Low German. One day a soldier heard me, and asked me where I was from. He, like me, was from Northern Germany.

He inquired, "Why are you going to all the trouble to harness those horses and drive around when there is no need for it? It is simply a waste of energy."

"I enjoy horses," I told him. "I do it for my own pleasure."

"How can you enjoy anything? Don't you realize we will be sent to a Russian prison? Don't you care? I have five children whom I'll never see again."

"Why do you say that? We probably won't be imprisoned for the rest of our lives."

"If we go to Siberia, our lives won't last very long."

"Well," I told him, "then we had better enjoy ourselves for whatever time we can."

Food would have been a frightful problem except for the horses. Every few days we butchered one of the them. On a day when I was butchering, we received an order from our company command to pack up and drive our half-track to the coast. Since food was always on my mind, I quickly quartered the horse and tossed it onto the platform of the half-track.

We got to the beach in the evening, and immediately I dug a little hole, put a piece of iron across it to make a stove, and began melting the fat from the interior of the horse. I knew that rendered fat would not spoil as quickly as meat.

I got about a quart of oily substance, for horse fat is thin. I poured it into my canteen and tied it to my belt. I barely finished by dark.

Unexpectedly, a ship had slipped into the harbor to evacuate us, and we were transported to it in small boats.

The sailors on the ship let a ladder down, and we were instructed to climb up.

When it comes to heights, I lose my courage. Anything higher than the back of a horse is too high for me, and I get dizzy.

As we neared the ship, a sailor yelled, "All lights out! There is danger of a Russian submarine in the area!"

"Oh boy," I thought. "It gets worse and worse."

I didn't see how I could climb that ladder under the best of circumstances, much less in the dark. Finally my turn came. The line of soldiers was moving up, and rung by rung, I moved with it. When I got to the top, two sailors grabbed me and pulled me over the rail. Actually, the darkness helped me, for I wasn't able to look down and see how high I was climbing.

Life jackets were handed out as we came on board. The third man in front of me got the last jacket. I wasn't upset about not getting one, for since I had never learned to swim, I had never become comfortable in water. If the ship went down, I figured I would drown quickly. I wouldn't be floating around on the vast ocean, wasting away and dying a slow, miserable death.

Oddly, dying no longer worried me, which was surprising because I am not a particularly brave man. However, we had been through a thousand disasters: we had fought on the front line for two and a half years, had been overpowered in battle, had suffered danger after danger on our long retreat, had been detained as prisoners on a peninsula, and now were on an overloaded ship. After a while, I began to feel that even though God was surely shielding me, my turn to bow out of this life could come any time. So be it. To depart by drowning wouldn't be as bad as some deaths I had witnessed.

The ship was ordinarily used to train newly recruited German sailors how to maneuver a vessel. The plan had been for the sailors to take on supplies at Copenhagen in preparation for a lengthy training session. The bread that was to be loaded was still hot. The captain decided to take the ship out for a brief lesson before loading supplies. Once out to sea, he got orders to come to the peninsula to evacuate soldiers.

We estimated that there were about 8000 soldiers packed on the ship. Because of the crowded condition, a few of us climbed a ladder to a high platform. Had the craft been rigged for battle, the platform would have had a gun mounted on it. We, a group of about five or six soldiers, claimed it as our special quarters for the nine days we were aboard the ship.

Since there was very little food, everyone was constantly hungry. Each day they served a little slimy water that was supposed to be soup, but actually was water with an unappetizing tan tint. The men were weak, and the crowded ship was hot. Sometimes people keeled over while they waited in the long line for their cup of soup. I, too, was unsteady and dizzy-headed which made it necessary for me to hold onto the railing while climbing the ladder to our platform.

However, in comparison to the others, we on the pedestal had an advantage. When we got our soup, I stirred a little of the horse fat into each cup. We still were sure we were starving, but we weren't quite as bad off as the other 7,995 soldiers on the ship. Of course, I thought often of the butchered horse we had abandoned on the platform of our half-track.

Finally we arrived at Kiel, a German seaport on the Baltic Sea. Because our ship was overloaded, we couldn't get into port. While we waited, a rumor began circulating aboard ship that the war was over. When a small boat came by with an older man and a teenager in it, we called out :

"Is it true that the war is over?"

"Yes, it's true."

"Well, how are things?"

The older man looked away and was silent. The boy answered. "Pretty good. But some of the girls are running around with American soldiers."

That bit of information was bitter medicine. In regard to the results of losing the war, it was the first discouragement we received.

The same day a small, one-seated, American plane flew over. The youthful pilot circled, revving the motor. He was grinning . . . goofing . . . gloating. With each revolution the plane dipped lower. Finally, as it banked, it came too low. It was sad. A tilted wing struck the water. Shoost! The plane and its pilot were gone.

Most of the 8000 men cheered. I felt it was true that the cocky kid deserved a sock in the jaw, but he didn't deserve to die. What a stupid waste! What a permanent price to pay for a few moments of arrogance! His own life was gone, and somewhere in the States he had a mother who would grieve for the rest of her days.

While we waited for a way to land, the ship settled low during ebb tide and hit bottom. In order to lighten it, the captain obtained a second vessel and transported some of the men onto it. Once more afloat, we were able to move to a landing site. Since we now were entering the English-occupied portion of Germany, we were told all weapons must remain aboard. Stubbornly, I decided that the enemy was not going to get my pistol. I took it apart, dividing it into small pieces. Fragment by fragment, I threw it into the sea.

We were unloaded and immediately sent to a barn on a nearby farm. Of course, to say we were hungry was an understatement. We were starved. The farmer had a huge kettle. He put chopped cabbage, kohlrabi, turnips--whatever he could find--into it and cooked it. It wasn't anything you or I would care to eat now, but the multitude of soldiers declared it was the finest meal they had ever eaten.

The farmer milked about twenty cows. When it was about chore time, four of us who had farm experience jumped up and milked the cows. We did his chores for about three weeks, freeing him to work at other jobs. We had an advantage, for we sometimes found it handy to shoot a stream of milk into our own mouths rather than into the bucket.

The British realized the value of providing food for

the populace and decided that any of us who could prove we had a farm connection would be freed first. The occupation given on my passport was *farmer*, and our farm was in the British Occupied Zone. I felt wonderfully blessed when I was one of the first soldiers freed to return to my family. Amazingly, I had survived the war.

On the first leg of the journey home, I rode in the back of a military truck with a canvas over the top. We stopped at a checkpoint where the driver showed identification. There I noticed that one of the guards was a black man. Since he was the first black person I had ever seen, I was fascinated. I was amazed that the whites of his eyes were especially noticeable because they contrasted with his skin. When he waved us on, I saw that the palms of his hands were a lighter color which was another surprise to me.

The truck stopped at Oldenburg, a town that was about forty kilometers from our farm. We all climbed out. One of my uncles, Siebelt Bless, lived there. Our truckload of soldiers was quite an attraction because we were the first prisoners freed. Each of us was wearing a yellow ribbon, a sign that we had been legally released.

Among the townsmen lining the streets to welcome us was my cousin, Helga Bless. We recognized each other, and as soon as I was given permission to leave the group, I went with her to my uncle's house. It was a happy reunion with additional good fortune, a home-cooked meal! The family ran a grocery store which meant they had food available.

I began to consider the best way to get to our farm, and again heaven smiled on me. My uncle's mother-in-law lived in the same hamlet as did my parents. She had ridden her bicycle to Oldenburg and had later gone home in the wagon with her husband, leaving her bicycle behind. My uncle had been wondering how to return it to her, and now he asked me to ride it home.

Part of the road was cobblestone and part was asphalt. However, I cycled beside the road on a dirt trail which was meant for pedestrians and bikers. As I rolled along, I worried about the best way to present myself to the family. The mail service had broken down, and I didn't know how many of my letters they had received. When I was on the peninsula, I had sent a letter with a civilian, hoping that it would be passed on to them. At the time I wrote, I was in danger of being sent to a Russian prison camp, and I had hinted so in my letter.

My sister, Henni, had a heart condition, a problem brought on by the stress of working in military hospitals. Once when I had come home on furlough and had walked into the house unannounced, it had been a terrible shock to her as well as to my mother. I didn't want to startle them again. When I neared the farm, I decided to cycle by to see if anyone might be outside.

As I whizzed past the buildings, I saw my dad and brother, Bernhard, closing a gate for the night.

"Good evening," I said cheerfully and pedalled on, immediately disappearing behind a thorny hedge. I stopped, turned around, and went back. Bernhard had recognized me.

After greeting me warmly, he said, "I'll go tell Mom!"

"Be careful not to startle her or Henni," I cautioned.

"I know what I'll do. We always let the servicemen who are trying to sneak home sleep in the barn. I'll tell Mom another soldier needs a sleeping place." He went inside.

"Mom," he said, "There's a soldier to stay the night. This one is really hungry, though, so you'll have to find something for him to eat."

I suppose that Bernhard's face was aglow, for when Mother looked up, she guessed the truth. "You can't fool me," she exclaimed." Heini is home!"

6
A Civilian Again

My mother called the girls who had already retired. By the time I entered the house, everyone was there to greet me. After I had eaten, Mom said, "Well, girls, we will have to make up another bed."

"No need for that!" I exclaimed. "I can't sleep in a bed!"

"Of course you can sleep in a bed," she said. "You're home now."

"But I have lice," I answered. "I can't sleep inside."

"Oh, no!" she exclaimed. "What are you sitting on?"

"On a wooden chair," I told her. "Not on anything upholstered."

I slept in the barn which was no great hardship. From March 4, 1944 until June 9, 1945, I had slept in a bed only three times.

The next morning I threw off my cover and went outside. Among my usual morning rituals was the task of stripping off my undershirt and examining it for lice. I found three of the little critters which I put under the face of my pocket watch where they would be handy to show my family.

We had a huge cast iron kettle that we used to cook food for the hogs. Mother scrubbed it, built a fire under it, and boiled all my clothes. She even boiled my leather goods. It ruined them, but she did get rid of the lice. Also, I scrubbed my body with a special solution.

Then another problem arose. I didn't have any civilian clothes. My old clothes didn't fit me because I had grown about two and a half inches while I was in the service. None of my brothers had extra clothes to loan me since scarcely any civilian goods had been manufactured in recent years. All energy and materials had gone into war products.

My mother and sisters were accomplished seamstresses. They used gunny sacks to make work clothes for me, but there were occasions when I needed something better than sack cloth garments.

I went to the ration center in town and managed to get a permit to buy clothes, but I was still faced with the problem of finding a merchant who had trousers or shirts for sale. Our nearest clothing store was empty except for a few black neckties. I left in disgust. A black necktie wouldn't go very well with a gunny sack shirt.

Dad said, "We'll go back. I'm sure he must have something for you."

"Yes," I said, chuckling. "Black neckties."

When we arrived at the store, Dad said, "This boy has been in the military, and he needs clothes. It just so happens that I recently butchered. We don't need all the meat."

Immediately the merchant was interested. "Come here," he said cheerfully. "We do have some merchandise for exchange."

He led us into a back room where there were racks of clothes. They weren't for sale for *money* because money was of no value at the time. But if a customer had a useful article to trade, he usually could make a deal. I got a pair of pants, a shirt, and a jacket.

As before the war, I returned to hard physical labor. I enjoyed it, but I was restless. Numerous horrible memories plagued my mind and interrupted my sleep. I went out socially after work and wasn't always careful about the company I kept. Sometimes I was pulled into activities that weren't exactly virtuous. I didn't break the law, but I surely did slide along the edge of it. The first months that I was home, the God that had shielded me in battle must have been a little disappointed in me.

One morning after I had been out late the night before, my dad talked to me about the direction my life was taking. He put a hand on my shoulder and said quietly, "You tell me the people you are associating with, and I'll tell you the kind of person you are."

These brief words set me to thinking. I knew he was right. I began attempting to make new friends whose favorite activities were more apt to coincide with mine.

One fall an evangelistic group came to our town for a week, and I attended the nightly services. It was a life-changing event, for I realized I must make a commitment to the Savior who had died for me. I noticed that my attitudes and my desires were now different. I began to live for the hereafter rather than for the moment. Since then, I have conducted my life accordingly.

I decided that the best way for me to get into farming on my own was to make contact with my uncle, Henry Bless, and go to America. In August, 1948, he came to Germany for a visit, and I had a chance to talk at length with him. Would the American citizens accept me, someone who had been their enemy in war? He told me Americans are warm, generous people. He felt that I wouldn't have a problem.

Heinrich and His Parents. Oct. 7, 1950. This picture was taken the night before Heinrich departed for America.

Soon I began to make the necessary plans. A thorough background check, probably made by the American Consulate, was necessary because the United States wished to keep Nazi war criminals from entering their country. Finally I got a reservation on a cargo ship out of Holland. On October 8, 1950, I went on the train to Bremen where I intended to buy a ticket into Holland. There a man approached me.

"Are you Mr. Cramer?" he asked.

At first I didn't trust him. However, he explained that he was from Bremen and was a passenger on the train as well as on the Dutch ship to America. He had gotten my name from the travel agency.

"There has been a change in plans," he told me. "Our ship has already departed from Holland and has gone to Belgium to take on more freight. When we get to Holland, we will have to take another train to Belgium." The station master confirmed his words. We stayed overnight in Holland where I had my first ride in a civilian automobile. We took a taxicab to the hotel.

There were twelve passengers on the ship plus two French priests, both of whom became terribly seasick. We ate in the dining room after the captain and crew had finished. The cook was a black man who wore a chef's hat, had curly black hair, and coal black eyes. Just as with the first colored man I had seen, his black hands with lighter palms fascinated me. Since the server was an Oriental man, I had further opportunity to observe the physical differences among the various races.

One morning when there was an especially rough sea, the cook showed himself to be a good fellow. The roll of the ship made my stomach more and more queasy. I decided to go outside to the middle of the craft where there was less motion. I braced myself against a solid object and tried to hold myself steady.

I wasn't aware that I was near the kitchen until a small window opened, and there stood the cook. He spoke to me, but I couldn't understand his language. He handed me a lemon and indicated to me that I should eat some of it. I'm not much for sour foods, but I cut it open and ate a little. I found that it did help.

We were approaching Boston. My mother had given me six teaspoons with a special design to give to my aunt. I was asked to fill out a piece of paper, list anything I had in my possession, and give its value. I listed the teaspoons but could only guess at their value because I had no idea. The man who was in charge spoke German, and he looked at my paper.

"Are the spoons really this valuable?" he asked.

"I have no idea," I answered.

"At that price, you'd have to pay quite a bit of toll on them," he said. "I don't think they are worth that much." He named a lower figure. I appreciated his help.

As we neared Boston, we were under strict surveillance. Someone followed all of us except the priests everywhere we went. They let the two priests off there, but the rest of us continued on to New York City. On Thursday I got off at Ellis Island where I was questioned. During that time three other people were in the room: a typist, an interpreter, and the questioner. After fifteen or twenty minutes, they dismissed me. There were a large number of other immigrants waiting to have their papers processed.

The next day they called me back. After more questions, a man said, "I hate to tell you this, but we may have to send you back to Germany."

"Fine," I said, shrugging.

"You mean that doesn't upset you?"

"No. My mom and dad didn't want me to come anyway. They would be glad to welcome me back. But I wish you would decide soon. I conquered my seasickness on the way over, and if I get back on the ship soon, perhaps I won't get so sick going home."

Most of the people who had arrived were displaced persons, and to be denied admittance would have been disastrous. Their European home was probably a tiny attic room with an orange crate for furniture. But I could return to my family. If I were sent back, I'd put on my wooden shoes, and I'd go out to help my dad.

I thought that my papers were completely in order, but the American government had changed the conditions regarding immigrants. My papers were not in line with the new rules. While we waited, we got good care on Ellis Island, but we had nothing to do.

Finally, I was called in for counseling. "How are things?" I was asked.

"Fine, except it is boring."

"Do you need anything?'

"No."

"Not anything?"

"No. We get good meals, a place to sleep, and clean towels every evening."

"Don't you need some money?"

"No. my uncle sent a few dollars and I can get by. The only thing I might need is a stamp to write a letter."

"It is my duty to tell you that you can request some money from the American government."

"I'm not going to request any money. I came here to work, not to beg."

He shook his head. "I never before saw a guy like you. You have the right to be paid while you are detained here."

"Why do I have the right?" I asked. "I didn't do any work for the government. They don't owe me anything." I was indignant.

It upsets me yet today to think about it. When people take from the government, it opens the door for the government to tell them what to do. People in this country talk about the government slowly taking their freedom. They are wrong. The government doesn't take their freedom. Rather, people give their freedom away by depending on the government.

In Germany people at first had rallied to Hitler's generous programs. By the time he had full power, he had the country by the throat. For instance, Dad had objected to the government's plan to draft fifteen-year-old Bernhard.

"I need him on the farm," Dad said. "We do considerable volunteer work for other families who are short of help since their men are in the service. I can't manage without him."

Their answer stunned my dad. They told him that the government had bought the right to the children long ago. Hadn't they faithfully made payments for each child that the family had produced? Happily, the war came to an end before Bernhard was inducted.

While I was on Ellis Island, some wealthy Germans came there. I didn't talk to them much because I felt plain and clumsy in their presence. However, they spoke fairly good English. I tried to get in the food line behind them so that I could listen to them and perhaps learn some English words.

I thought I knew how to express gratitude in English, and whenever I was served a food item, I said, 'Thank you." Then I heard the German couple say some extra syllables after the phrase. I worried that I was speaking incorrectly and quit saying it. In thinking back, they probably said, "Thank you very much,"

By Wednesday, all but about 40 or 50 people had been dismissed from the island. Late that afternoon, I was notified that I was free to go. However, I would be on six month's probation. Also, the baggage room had already been locked, and since the next day was Thanksgiving, the baggage man wouldn't be back until Friday. I would have to come back on Friday for my luggage.

"You are free to go tonight if you have friends or relatives in New York where you can stay for a couple of days. If you haven't, you might as well stay here." Of course, I stayed, but it was a long holiday for me. I had received word that Uncle Henry had been injured in a fire and consequently needed help on his farm.

The time during the Thanksgiving break seemed endless. I fretted about my uncle who had received severe burns on sixty percent of his body. Also, since he was in the hospital, there would be no one to direct me in learning how to do his farm work. He had a tractor, a machine with which I was totally inexperienced. I worried that I wouldn't be able to communicate with his wife. She probably spoke only English, a language I didn't yet know.

After getting my luggage Friday morning, I was sent on a small boat to the mainland. A taxi driver who spoke a little German approached me and asked, "Are you Mr. Cramer?"

"Yes, I am."

"All right. I'll take you to the train depot."

Once in the railroad station, he warned me to keep an eye on my luggage which consisted of one suitcase.

"Your train will leave about seven o'clock from Track 12," he told me. "You sit right here and wait. If anyone comes along and wants to talk to you, don't answer. Don't trust anyone. When you need to eat, go to this counter right here to get something."

About noon I approached the counter. I had rarely eaten in a restaurant, even in Germany. A girl with a white apron put a menu in front of me, but I couldn't read it. She came back and said something, but I couldn't understand. A second girl joined her. They tried to talk to me, but their language might as well have been Greek.

They left and soon a fellow in a chef's cap came. After trying to talk to me in English, he switched to German. "Where did you arrive from?" he asked.

Now I could understand! "Ellis Island," I answered.

"I believe you came to eat, didn't you?"

"Yes, I did."

"I'll get you something."

In a short time, one of the girls brought a big plateful of food. There were large portions of meat, potatoes, and vegetables. Oh, boy! I wasn't *that* hungry, but a young fellow likes to eat. Man! This was really living it up. And it cost me only one dollar! America, I love you!"

Part Two
Henry

7
Behind the Windbreak

In the evening I got on the train. It was snowing and blowing and was freezing cold in the unheated car. I was unable to see outside through the frosted windows. However, when the train stalled because of the snow, I blew on the window until there was a clear space which allowed me to peek out. I saw a small, shriveled pony hunched in the storm. Disappointed, I shook my head and thought, "It's Russia all over again!"

Finally, in spite of the storm, we made it to Chicago. There were three Rumanian men on the train who spoke a little German. They had come to America as displaced persons, and like me, had an overnight layover in Chicago. The people who sponsored their trip had hired a lady to meet the train and assist them. Even though I was with them, she at first ignored me. However, she apparently reconsidered, for she finally offered to help me, also. She told me which train I should take the next day to get to Columbus. That night two of the Rumanians, a father and son, slept in one room, and the third slept with me in another.

The next morning the son and I went down the hall to take baths. He wanted to get back into his room, but the door was locked. He knocked repeatedly, but his father was partially deaf and was sound asleep. The son asked me what to do.

We went down to the desk where I spoke to the

clerk in the three languages I knew: Low German, High German, and Russian. Finally, probably more through gestures than speech, I was able to convey the idea that we needed another key.

Once back on the train and headed for Nebraska, I decided that, even though I needed to be careful with my funds, I had better eat again. I hadn't eaten anything since the meal in New York which was two days before. I don't recall what I ordered, but it was a small amount, hardly enough to fill a hollow tooth. It cost more than two dollars! I was disbelieving since I had eaten a fabulous meal in New York City for one dollar. I decided that I wouldn't eat any more food on the train.

Before I left Germany, I had visited a friend. His mother inquired about my plans to go to America. When she learned where I was going, she exclaimed, "Columbus, Nebraska! I have a first cousin living there."

She gave me his address, and I corresponded with him. He sent his telephone number, and said that when I arrived, I should call him and he'd pick me up from the station. I wrote my uncle about the man, and he replied, "When you get here, I will pick you up from the station. There is no need to ask anyone else to meet you."

Of course, since my uncle was in a hospital, I was glad that I had the address of the fellow in Columbus. The distance across this wide land was a surprise to me, but finally about midnight the train arrived. I was the only passenger getting off. The depot was quiet except for a couple young fellows who were coming in and out. I showed the station master my paper with the telephone number on it. He tried to call, but no one answered.

Then suddenly, the two young fellows grabbed my suitcase and went out. I was intensely aware that during the war I had been the enemy, and was uncertain and anxious about their motives. Not knowing what else to do, I followed them. They put my suitcase in a car and motioned for me to get in also. Who were they? Why had they taken my suitcase? Where were they taking me? Reluctantly, I got in.

They drove to the outer edge of Columbus, stopped in a yard, and got out. They ushered me to the entrance and knocked. No one answered. They opened the door, walked across the porch, and knocked on the next door. No answer. They unlatched that door and yelled inside. Soon a sleepy lad came downstairs. I got the impression that the boys knew each other, and that this was the destination I sought. Of course, we couldn't converse because of the language barrier.

Shortly after midnight the parents came home, and they could speak German. It was an immense relief to me to be able to talk to someone and to realize that they were glad to see me. They said they had stayed home every night for five weeks, thinking I would be coming. Then they decided to give up and go out for an evening, and it happened to be the very night that I came.

They knew my uncle's farm was nine miles west of Madison, and the next morning after breakfast, we set out. My aunt Lizzie saw the car coming down the long driveway. When I got out, she was standing on the porch holding the door open. I was overwhelmed with joy when she spoke to me in Low German.

"I'm so glad you are here!" In one instant tons of weight melted from my shoulders. How enjoyable it was to be able to communicate! She would be the one directing me until my uncle got out of the hospital.

Later I learned my uncle had been in a fire one cold morning when he flooded his tractor. He was testing a spark plug, and the gas, which had spilled because of the flooding, ignited. His clothes caught afire, and he was badly burned. He was hospitalized for months.

I looked around and decided what to do. I bypassed the tractor and harnessed a team of horses. My uncle had recently torn down an old barn and had built a new one which meant there was considerable cleaning up that needed to be done.

"The horses don't understand German," Aunt Lizzie said when I came in for supper.

"They did everything I asked," I answered.

The first time my cousin, Norman Bless, came home for a week end, he suggested that perhaps I could change my name, Heinrich, to its English counterpart, Henry. I thought it a good idea. In one word, I could proclaim my intentions of being an American. I became Henry.

The wealth of machinery in the farmyard was an amazement to me. The only farm machines I had operated in Germany had been the sickle mower and the plow. Here there were a dozen machines that were a mystery and a wonder. Would I actually be able to operate the incredible mazes of wheels, gears, bars, and levers?

The greatest handicap continued to be the feeling that I had recently been the enemy. During the war I did not personally fight against the Americans, but I would have done so had I been assigned to the western sector instead of the eastern. Whenever I met a new person, I wondered how he perceived me? Did he still think of me as the enemy?

Learning a fourth language was another difficulty, but I remembered the words of my teacher: "You can do it!" As I said before, they had become words to live by.

After I had been in the country about three weeks, I met a neighbor at the mailbox. He asked me about my uncle. With gestures and the use of the few English words that I knew, I tried to explain. I held out my arm, and stiffened my elbow. "Elbow." I said.

"How long have you been in America?" he asked.

I held up three fingers. "Three weeks," I told him.

"Three weeks!" he exclaimed. "You speak English so well. *Elbow*, yet!"

I found his comment encouraging. I didn't explain how I happened to know an unusual word like "elbow." It is the same in German as it is in English.

It was a frightening experience to be on probation for six months. Having lived under a dictatorship for most of my life, I knew all about governmental surveillance. Now I constantly wondered where the spying officers were located. Behind buildings or haystacks? In groves? I decided that in the area of the farmyard, the windbreak was the most likely place. Often I glanced that direction to see if I could detect movement behind it. Were eyes staring through the knotholes? How big of a mistake did a person have to make in order for them to write it down and report it? Or did they report all my activities? It never once occurred to me that in America, no one was watching.

My uncle had made arrangements for a part-time job for me with Norman Praeuner who lived between Newman Grove and Battlecreek, and in February I began working there. I sometimes returned to help my aunt, however, for my uncle remained in the hospital. Fortunately, both families had John Deere tractors, and Norman began teaching me about the use of a tractor. He couldn't speak much German, but he would show me while I watched carefully.

When we hauled hay, I noticed that he sometimes put the tractor out of gear and let it coast downhill. Near the bottom, he slipped it back in gear just in time for the motor to catch. One day he sent me to his dad's place to get a load of shelled corn. I was driving a 36 B John Deere which was pulling a flare box wagon. With a heavy load on, I headed for home.

As I came over the crest of a hill, I shoved the tractor out of gear. It didn't take long for me to realize that I had made a serious error. I said, "Lord, if you let me make it safely to the bottom, I will never do that again!" He heard me, and I survived. Then I glanced around. Where was the surveillance officer stationed, I wondered, and what did he write in his book?

I recall once when I was discing. Norman told me, "When you get to the end, don't turn too short, or the wheel will catch the tongue. But don't leave too much space, either." He walked away and never looked back. Oh, I was scared. He had said, "Turn short, but don't turn too short." My worry was made worse by the fellow that I supposed was behind the windbreak. However, all went well.

I returned to my uncle's farm to disc cornstalks and

seed oats. I used an end gate seeder, a device fastened in the back of a wagon. The horses were a well-trained team, and when I got them started down the row, I tied the lines and jumped to the ground. Using a five gallon bucket of seed oats, I sowed a strip beside the wagon by hand. We always sowed by hand in Germany.

My uncle had yard scales in the farmyard. One morning a neighbor came over to weigh something. When he saw me coming home from the field, he asked my aunt, "What's he doing out there?"

"He's coming home from sowing a load of oats."

"He's sowed a load already? I'm just ready to start."

When Aunt Lizzie told me about it, I thought about the man that I supposed was lurking behind the windbreak. I hoped that if he reported my unusual method of sowing grain, he considered it a plus rather than thinking I was overdoing it.

When I was in the post office buying stamps, the postal clerk gave me too much change. I shoved some back and said, "I believe you gave me too much." I wondered if he had been asked by the surveillance team to test my honesty. It was a great relief when the six months of probation were over.

Because of the distance between my two jobs and also to town, I wanted to get a car. I still owed my uncle $300.00 for my ticket to America, but I felt I needed a way of transportation. Norman and I went to Madison on the eighth of April, and I bought a '36 Ford, a car that was fifteen years old. I could hardly imagine! I had left Germany only six months before and now I owned a car. It cost seventy-five dollars. When I cleaned it, I found thirty-six cents under the seat. The car actually cost me only seventy-four dollars and sixty-four cents!

Periodically I went to Newman Grove for a haircut. Since I was insecure about driving, I parked at the edge of town and walked to the barber shop. I hadn't yet felt confident enough to apply for a driver's license.

I had eaten bananas in salads, but otherwise I had never eaten one as a fruit. In Europe the fruits we had were ones we raised ourselves, and that didn't include bananas. I wanted to try one. On a Saturday night I walked into a grocery store and bought three over-ripe bananas for five cents. I was not disappointed in their taste, for they were delicious. I ate all three. I drove home feeling guilty, however, because I had spent five cents unnecessarily when I still owed my uncle.

The day came when I decided I must get my driver's license. I drove to the courthouse in Madison, but it was closed until noon. While I waited, I went to visit one of my Uncle's friends. When it was time for me to return to the courthouse, he said, "One of the boys will go with you. If the patrolman asks how you got here, you won't have to reveal that you drove without a license."

The written exam came first. Since I couldn't read much English, my companion read the questions for me while the patrolman kept a close eye on us. Then the officer took me out to the car for the driver's test. My friend was going to accompany us, but the officer told him to wait at the courthouse.

"I think the two of us will get along okay," he said.

He told me to make a right turn. I was nervous, and signalled for a left turn.

"I said right turn!" he repeated.

I corrected my mistake. We drove for awhile.

"How is the hand brake?" he asked.

"That thing doesn't work," I told him.

He directed me to make another turn which took us back to the courthouse. We went inside where he filled out a card which the mechanic was to sign after he repaired the hand brake.

"When you return this card, you can pick up your driver's license," he told me. I had successfully crossed another hurdle.

When threshing time came, it was a picnic for me. I loved it! In Germany we hauled bundles on a wheel barrow. Here we used a team and wagon which made it fun.

One day we were threshing for Norman's parents.

Norman's brother, Carl, who had been seriously injured in the war, lived there. Since I had fought on the opposing side, I was afraid the family would be angry with me. When we entered the house for the noon meal, I was shaking from head to toe.

You can imagine my relief when the injured man approached me, put an arm around my shoulders, and told me that he knew I wasn't the one who had shot him. He said that even if I had been, he wouldn't blame me because it was a situation where each of us did what we could to survive. I was overjoyed at his forgiving attitude.

After I got my car, I occasionally visited a lovely couple in the neighborhood, Campbell and Elizabeth Brown. Elizabeth was a school teacher and gave me my first lessons in reading and writing English. Sometimes I picked up a couple of her nephews who lived nearby and took them along. It was a pleasant social evening where I learned many things about life in America along with a better way of speaking English. I am forever grateful to her for her generous, time-consuming assistance.

I worked part-time for Norman Praeuner until my cousin, Norman Bless, graduated from the University, after which I worked full time for Praeuners. Whether I worked at Praeuners or for my uncle, my wages were a dollar a day. When corn picking time came, I was paid $100.00 a month.

Another fellow wanted to hire me, but I felt obligated to stay with Praeuners. Then the other man said, "Do you have a brother? I'd be glad to sponsor him if he'd come to America and work for me." This remark gave me confidence. Maybe I was doing all right after all.

Comments by Norman Praeuner who now lives in Battle Creek:

Henry's Uncle and my father-in-law, Arthur Just, were good friends. I needed help because we were moving to a larger farm. Henry, along with some of my neighbors and relatives, came to help. We got quite a few things loaded and went inside for dinner. We found out that a snowstorm was forecast for the next day.

My dad and brother, Carl, decided we should complete as much of the moving as possible that afternoon. Henry set off for the new place with a team and a load of oats. Some of the neighbors followed with household items. When he arrived, Henry unloaded the oats after which he helped the other men unload the furniture.

When my wife, Adelyn, came later, she found that Henry had located some rusty stovepipe, had set up the cooking stove, and had built a fire. The kitchen was warm and the teakettle was merrily boiling. What a relief for a tired woman who had to produce supper for the men!

I had 170 head of livestock which we moved that afternoon. The fences on our new place were in terrible shape, and we never could have managed without Henry. He went to work on the fence and patched it up.

Later the landlord, who was anxious to have the fences well repaired, furnished posts and wire, With Henry's help, we did a good job. The landlord bought a post hole digger that fit my John Deere tractor and loaned it to us. My new hired man adapted to everything quickly and was soon running the tractor and digger like he'd done it all his life.

Henry had a strict sense of honesty. He told me one day that when it rained so we couldn't work in the field, he would like for me to show him how to service the tractor and other machinery. He said that on those days he wouldn't expect to be paid. He was mechanically inclined and caught on fast.

Henry broke the handle on a corn knife. He found a piece of a pitchfork handle, and used it to make a handle for the corn knife. We have that old corn knife with the home-made handle yet today.

In the spring when Henry bought his car, Adelyn drove our car home, and I drove Henry's car. I had planned to take him out in the pasture that evening to *give him a driving lesson, but we had company. After awhile, we heard the motor start and the sound of the car leaving the place. Henry had watched me so carefully on the way home that he was able to start the car and drive to the neighbors by himself. We were surprised that he had learned so quickly.*

Once Henry and I were hauling baled hay, using a tractor and a wagon with a flat rack. We got a puncture in a tire on the wagon. A neighbor came along and I rode with him to a nearby farm where I hoped to borrow the things we needed to fix the flat. No one was home, and we returned to our stalled vehicle.

Upon arriving, I found that Henry had blocked the tires of the wagon to keep it from rolling and had driven away with the tractor. I was surprised because I didn't know that he knew how to operate that particular tractor. He had gone to ask another neighbor for help. He returned with a lug wrench, a wheel, a tire, and a jack. We had everything we needed to get the wagon back in operation.

Henry was an excellent hired man. He gave his entire attention to a task, had a good character, was handy with both machines and animals, and had a refreshing sense of humor.

Henry Continues:

In November, Norman Praeuner informed me that I could stay for the winter if I chose, but he didn't need a hired man, and thus wouldn't be able to pay me wages.

"When spring work commences," he said, "I will again put you on the payroll." I decided it best to look for another job.

My cousin, Norman Bless, told me about a job on a dairy farm near Omaha. The following Sunday, a friend and I went to Omaha. George Sorenson of Sorenson's Dairy, 66th and Redick, agreed to hire me. I was to begin on December first and would be paid $150 per month plus room and board.

8
Esther

I had never before operated a milking machine, but I learned quickly. Within a week George designated a string of cows for me to milk night and morning. Shortly thereafter, he raised my wages to $175 a month.

I was happy with the work, but I had a problem. There were five other milkers, all of them pleasant fellows, and we lived together. I was learning to speak English, and those young men didn't set the best example for me. I sometimes discovered that a word I had learned was one that shouldn't have been in my vocabulary.

I recall an amusing incident. Once I commented that I had a headache. One of the other workers gave me a medication. It looked like a small glass bulb with grains of something in it. On closer examination, I decided it perhaps was a plastic bulb, but whether glass or plastic, it surely wasn't edible. I opened it, spilled the grains into my hand, and swallowed them. It was the first time I had seen medicine in a capsule.

For the sake of controlling the direction of my growing vocabulary, I decided I needed to be associating with Christian people. Early in April I asked Bud Parker, who attended the same church I did, if he knew of a farmer who needed help.

"If you're looking for a job, I can use you," he said.

"I don't know anything about your kind of business," I told him. He ran a Skelly Service Station and a Case Machinery business.

"Then you're the person I want," he said. "I can teach you what I choose."

I found that, with a seven-to-five work day, I had too much free time. By then I was acquainted with Art Camenzind, a Swiss German who lived in Irvington. His business was buying and selling dairy cows. He hired me to work for him part time, mornings and evenings, and invited me to live with him, his wife Luanna, and their two small children. All went well for a time, but eventually, I found that the hours from my two jobs were now too long. I was wearing down.

In the fall Art employed me full-time. I worked on the selling end of the business. I paid close attention to Art's remarks about the various cows and the prices he expected to get for them. When a customer came, I tried hard to sell a cow, and often I got the job done.

Art never criticized me. Both Art's parents and Luanna's parents accepted me as one of the family and invited me to various family activities.

Some remarks by Art Camenzind who continues to live in Omaha:

Henry worked here for a total of about seven years. From the very beginning, he and I saw things alike. I admired his conservative, common-sense approach to any problem. Also, he was good at organizing.

Often I was away from home buying or delivering dairy cows and calves. When I'd come home, I always found everything in good order. I would ask Henry, "What needs to be done next around here? How can I help?" He, the hired man, would direct me!

We enjoyed watching him learn the language and the ways in our country. Once he needed to eat in a restaurant. After studying the menu, he finally recognized a word he knew, chicken. He indicated his choice to the waitress. When she brought him steak, he was perplexed. He thought he had ordered chicken. Actually he had ordered chicken fried steak.

One time Henry was milking a shorthorn cow by hand. She was a well-trained cow, but something frightened her and she kicked the heck out of him. Since her sudden attack took him by surprise, it knocked him over. After he was down, she kept kicking. We were all concerned, but he came crawling out of the barn with

nothing more than some bad bruises.
Henry was a hard worker. He always had the good of the company in mind, and he got along well with our customers. Everyone liked Henry.

Comments by George Lund, Blair Nebraska.

When we lived in Irvington, we were good friends with Henry. He was in and out of our house like one of our own kids. He called me Uncle George. I recall that when I sold my cattle, Henry groomed them to make them "look pretty."
Henry is a good fellow, a good Christian man.

Henry continues his story:

While I was working there, a man came to talk to Art. Art had to leave the conversation to help a customer, and the fellow and I chatted. He commented that he had not participated in the war because he was a Mennonite and didn't believe in war. I didn't know anything about the Mennonites except that they sent care packages to Germany after the war.

In Germany the only people I knew who refused to engage in war were the Jehovah Witnesses. During World War II, they were rounded up and sent to concentration camps where they died. I didn't know what to think about this young Mennonite.

He mentioned Grace Bible Institute in Omaha and spoke of a German man who was attending it. He told me I should get in touch with the man, Gerhard Fast.

In the evening I called Gerhard, and we had a wonderful conversation. He, his wife Ruby, and I have remained staunch friends to this day. I felt drawn to attend Grace Bible School in spite of the fact that a part of me rebelled against it. What could I be thinking? The classes were taught in a language that was strange to me, I had been out of school for sixteen years, and I had never liked studying. As I enrolled, I thought I surely must be crazy.

The main value of the school was that I was associating with admirable people and was learning more English. I ran out of funds after three semesters and was forced to quit.

Next I went to Oklahoma to the "Go-Ye Mission." They had a dairy, and I was hired as the manager. I became acquainted with a young lady, Esther Smithermann, who worked there. We fell in love, got engaged, and returned to Omaha to marry on May 18, 1956.

Esther's grandparents had settled in the Carolinas. At age seventeen, her father went to California where he got a job on a railroad. Later he married and bought a ten-acre orange ranch. He died in the 1940's, leaving Gladys with five children.

Esther, the oldest child of John and Gladys May (Stingley) Smithermann, was born on February 29, 1924, at Corvina, California. She had two brothers, Robert and Thomas, and a sister, Gertrude. After graduating from La Puente High School, Esther attended the Bible Institute of Los Angelus (1942-1945). She then worked for Dun & Bradstreet as a secretary.

Later she got a position at the "Go-Ye Mission" in Eastern Oklahoma where she worked for over ten years. It was there that we met.

Even though Esther was the oldest child, she was the last to marry, possibly because she was the one who took care of the younger children and ran the household while her mother worked to support the family. After Esther and I married, she and her brothers and sister bought a mobile home for their mother who, up until that time, had lived a difficult life.

I got a job delivering packages for the big stores in Omaha. One day we got an urgent call for a quick delivery. The WOW Television Station needed a gown immediately. I was surprised when my superior chose me for the job.

Henry and Esther (Smithermann) Cramer. May 18, 1956.

"Of the people on hand at the moment, I think you are the most capable," he said. My eyes widened when he added, "Forget about speed limits and get this package there!" Usually, I'm not one to break the law, but this time I drove to make the trip as quickly as possible. I arrived on time and without mishap.

At first, Esther and I lived in Omaha. Then I found an acreage, and we moved to it. We had a few cows which we milked night and morning.

I needed more funds to get into farming on my own. I took a job at the packing plant because wages were better there. At first I guided carcasses into the cooler, but I knew the knife workers were getting paid more money. During coffee breaks, I went onto the floor and helped with the skinning in order to learn how to do it. When a skinning job opened up, I was ready and was hired.

Our first child was expected in May. I wanted it to be born into a home that was completely American, and I studied diligently in preparation for becoming a citizen. Paul was born on May 16, 1957, to two proud American parents, for I had become a citizen on April 17.

While I was working in the packing plant, we got a devastating letter from my mother. It contained the news that my father had suddenly died. Oh, I was laid low. It was as if I'd been mowed off at the ankles. I seemed not to have the ability to lift hand or foot. To make matters worse, he had been buried two weeks before she wrote. My brothers and sisters had wanted to notify me immediately, but Mother kept insisting that she should be the one to tell me. I guess she couldn't bring herself to do it sooner.

He had died of a heart attack. At that time, my parents were living with my brother and his family. In such a situation, it was the common practice for the mother-in-law to do the cooking and for the daughter-in-law to do the chores. In the evening Dad wasn't feeling well. He walked through the kitchen and said to Mom, "I'm going out to feed the calves. I'll be back in a little while. Since I don't feel the best, don't make me any fried potatoes for supper tonight." When he didn't return, Mom went out and found him lying in the feed house. He was dead. It was March 31, 1958.

I had previously written to my father about the family estate. Since I had left the country, I told him he needn't honor the law stating that the family farm should pass to the eldest son. Rather, I told him he should consider the family he had in Germany, and decide how he wished to handle his affairs in regard to them. Even though I had relinquished my property rights, my family asked me to come to Germany to help settle the estate.

I arrived in my old homeland October 8th, 1958, exactly eight years after I had departed. Everyone in the family was there except my youngest brother, Enno, who was working in Africa. After a few marvelous weeks, I returned to Nebraska.

Esther's mother hoped we would decide to move to California. She came to visit us in the spring of 1960, and we took her back by car. We were there two weeks after which I told her it wasn't a place where I cared to live.

"I want to be a farmer," I said, "and I can't do it here." She was disappointed, but she understood.

Esther and I decided to send Mathilde tickets to visit us in America. She was here for four months, and during that time our second child, Ruth Ann, was born, arriving on September 26, 1959.

Art Camenzind had bought a farm and he kept asking me to work for him. I resisted because of the money involved, for I could make more at the packing plant. Finally, after I'd been in the packing plant for four years, he raised his offer to the point where I thought it advantageous to work for him. I told him, though, that the following year I intended to quit.

"Why?" he asked. "What do you plan to do?"

"We intend to rent a farm and operate on our own," I said.

In the meantime, on February 15, 1961, our youngest child, Mark, joined us. Shortly thereafter, my mother came to visit. She was in America for six months, a part of the time with us and a part of the time with her brother, Henry Bless.

She liked America, but language was a problem. Esther didn't speak German. Sometimes they both thought they had communicated, but when they each repeated their understanding of the conversation to me, they often had been talking about totally different subjects. It was comical. However, both were sincerely caring people and all went well. My mother enjoyed her grandchildren. She carried Baby Mark around and said, "This little guy and I understand each other." Of course, she couldn't converse with the older children.

She especially enjoyed ice cream. In Germany at that time, there was scarcely any refrigeration in the homes, making ice cream a rare luxury. In the evening Esther sometimes told me to ask Mother if there was anything else she would like. Mother would smile sweetly and whisper, "Ice." That was one word she knew! We understood that she meant "ice cream."

Esther's mother died in 1962. Esther went to California for the funeral. The neighbors helped me with the children, and also with farm chores because I had a broken leg at the time. A two-year-old colt that I was training had kicked me in the leg.

One disagreeable, cold evening, a neighbor teasingly told me, "Esther is going to call one of these nights and say the weather is wonderful in sunny California, and she is going to stay there."

In a short time Esther called to tell me she was anxious to get home. As for the weather, she reported it was damp and chilly in California. Apparently, she had adjusted to Nebraska's more severe climate. She was a city lady who probably found life on a Nebraska farm difficult, but being a dedicated wife and mother, she considered her family above everything else.

Esther didn't help with the outside work. My philosophy was that if I couldn't make enough money to support the family, I should look for a different job. Esther had the children and the house to care for, and she kept the account books. Because of my foreign background, I thought it best if she handled the writing part of our business. She did an excellent job. During that time I didn't write a single check.

We continued to look at vacant farms. Finally, Art bought a farm near Papillion and offered to rent it to us on a cash basis. He wanted more rent than we were willing to pay, but after three months of negotiations, he came down to a figure that we felt was acceptable. We moved to it in November, 1961.

We operated a Grade A dairy on 140 acres of land. We started with nothing, but Esther got $10,000 after her dad's property in California was sold. She generously shared her money, and we used it to buy dairy cows. We grew alfalfa and corn, both of which I chopped or put into silage. We fed chopped alfalfa even in the summer because our forty head of cows produced more milk on it than they did on pasture.

Paul worked with me from the time he was a preschooler. He rode on the tractor with me and when I got off to open a gate, he drove the tractor and the feed wagon through the gate. When he was a little older, I let him pull the loads of feed while I went ahead to begin chores. I could trust him to use the gear I suggested and to follow my directions to the letter, no questions asked.

When Mark reached the age when he was beginning to drive for me, he, too, was good about following my orders exactly, but he always had suggestions or questions.

Once he said, "Dad, if I'd have come in a faster gear, I'd have reached the milk house sooner to help you with chores. Besides, it would have saved gas." The boys not only were a great help, but they amused me. Both of them loved machinery and eventually were good at making needed repairs.

Later I learned that Ruth Ann envied the boys their opportunity to work outside. She would have enjoyed working with me also, but I usually told her she should help her mother in the house. It just didn't occur to me that she might prefer working outside a part of the time.

The kids each had their turn at helping me get the cows into the barn at milking time. A child waited outside, and when I turned two cows out of the milking barn, they eased two more in. Then they had to wait until I turned another pair out. It was a boring, tiring, one-and-a half or two-hour job, but they didn't complain.

I've always been proud of my children. I recall hearing an old saying that a son is a man's pride, and a daughter is his joy. By now, I can understand the truth in those words.

**Children of
Henry and Esther:
Paul, 14;
Ruth Ann, 12;
Mark, 10.
1971**

When the boys were teenagers, they obtained an old car, and brought it home. They spent days overhauling it. I couldn't help them because I didn't know anything about motors. When they were finished, they started it and drove away. It functioned fine for a while and then quit. They had made the bearings too tight and had burned the motor out. It was a good education for them. Now either boy can repair almost anything on a vehicle.

After we had been there eleven years, the farm programs, such as set-aside acres, came into being. I was strictly against taking money from government organizations. They would pay me not to produce? They would pay me not to work? I wanted no part of such an arrangement.

We in America enjoy unparalleled freedoms. People here complain that the government is slowly eroding these freedoms. It is not true. The people, rather, are *giving away* their freedoms by taking hand-outs from the government. By similar methods, Hitler bought the freedom away from his people.

The Communists continue to be oppressive. They take everything from everyone and promise each a fair share in the redistribution. But it doesn't happen that way, and people lose their incentive to work if they can't enjoy the fruits of their labor.

I refused to participate in any of the subsidy programs. However, because of the government payments to other farmers, rent went up to a figure that I couldn't afford. We sold out. We had a dairy sale on Monday and an equipment sale on Saturday.

For a while I worked for Larry Schram, a neighbor who operated feedlots. Then Esther heard that two brothers, Warren and Lyle Nelson, in Dannebrog had a dairy and were looking for a herdsman. I called one of them on the telephone and asked when I could come down to get acquainted with them.

He said, "We don't need to get acquainted. I've heard about you. We would like you to manage our herd. When can you come?"

"My boss is on vacation," I told him. "Of course, I need to give him a couple week's notice."

"But we need you tomorrow," he stated.

"Okay. If you insist, I'll come tomorrow, but only on these terms: When I feel like quitting, I will tell you the night before that I am leaving in the morning."

"Well, all right," he said. "Take all the time you need."

About a year and a half earlier, we had become acquainted with the pastor in the Baptist Church in Dannebrog. Now we went to visit him. He asked if there was anything he could do to help us move. I thought about it, then said, "Well, would you be willing to move us the German way?"

"Sure!" he said. "How is that?"

I told him that in Germany the residents from the new neighborhood come to get the people who are moving. The old neighbors don't help because their actions might be construed to mean that they are glad to see their neighbor leave."

On Sunday, he announced our plans in church. He asked for trucks, pickups, and manpower. The people were generous in responding, and we were soon moved.

We lived in Dannebrog for three years. I milked about 110 cows twice a day, beginning my day at 3:30 A.M. Paul graduated from Centura, a school that serves three towns: Cairo, Boelus, and Dannebrog.

When Ruth Ann was a high school sophomore, Esther decided she wanted to visit North Carolina, the place where her father was born. As far as she knew, her father had never returned for a visit after he left as a teenager. She had an aunt living in that area. While she was gone, Ruth Ann did a wonderful job running the household. When I came inside from morning chores, I found a note telling me exactly what was available for me to eat while she was in school. After supper each evening, she washed dishes and made plans for the next day. We were immensely proud of her and saved some of those notes. One is reprinted on the next page.

3-5-75

Howdy!
Ready for breakfast? Your potatoes are in the frig on the top shelf, waiting to be cut up and eaten. Use the small frying pan, already on the stove. Pour a little tiny bit of oil in the bottom of pan, then cut up the potatoes. Have burner on about Med Hi, or around there.

Now for your lunch.... there's the makings for sandwiches in the frig, along with some Cheerry Jello on the bottom shelf. The cake is on the wood stove. (Have as much cake as you want, cuz I'll make some more for tomorrow, and I don't want any more.)

Here's what you do for Supper... About 20 minutes till 4:00, turn on the oven to bake. (Check the degrees to make sure it's set on 225°.) Next take out the T.V. dinners on the top racks in the freezer. On the chicken one, be sure to cut open the place for dessert. Don't worry about setting the clock, cuz if you just turn the oven on, and put the dinners in, everything will be ready when we get home.

So much for your assignment for the day. Leave your dishes in the sink, and I'll do them when I get home.

See ya later...

Love,
R.A.

Since there was no opportunity for young people to get jobs in the area, we moved (in the spring of 1976) to a house on Kremer Farms seven miles south of Aurora. I worked as a hired man there. Ruth Ann graduated from Aurora High school in 1977 and Mark in 1979.

Then disaster struck. We learned that Esther had pancreatic cancer. Finally, since I was spending a considerable amount of time at the hospital with her, I lost my job. She died June 22, 1981.

My life was shattered. Simultaneously, I had lost my wife, my job, and our home, for the house was connected with the job. I felt like a wilting, uprooted plant--like a piece of driftwood that was tossing in an ocean--like an old chair with two missing legs. I could rejoice because Esther was in a happier place and free of pain. But me? Would I ever stand up and face the world again?

At the time of Esther's death, Paul and his wife Jamie (Proffitt) were in the US Navy. Ruth Ann had married David Wyatt, and was the mother of our first grandson, Aaron. Mark was working for a farmer near Aurora. During those first weeks, he spent many hours with me.

9
Life Goes On

Through faith in God and the help of my children, I became aware that the grass continued to grow and the sky was still blue. With Mark's encouragement, I bought an eight-acre place north of Aurora and moved onto it. (Later I sold two of the acres). For a while I had no job. Perhaps it was as well, for I could think of nothing but Esther. Finally, though, I realized I needed to be busy.

By now, three different people had offered me jobs involving selling. I could sell insurance, cemetery monuments, or animal feeds. Since I liked farming and animals, I decided to try being a feed salesman. I had enjoyed selling dairy cows for Art, but in that situation, customers had come to his place of business. Now in selling feed, I would have to visit various farmers and try to interest them in our brand of feed.

Bob Tams was the founder and owner for that particular feed company, and I went to him.

"If you ride with me to various farms in the neighborhood," I told him, "perhaps I can determine if I want to do this kind of work."

He stayed with me a few days and we travelled around telling farmers about his products. I decided I'd give the job a try. He gave me literature and samples of the different kinds of feed that he handled. Mostly, he dealt in pig feeds and cattle minerals.

Initially, when I approached a farmer and told him what I was doing, I was relieved if he said he wasn't interested. Then I didn't have to attempt to explain our various products. However, if I came upon someone who was interested, I would say, "I'm new at this business. I don't know much about these feeds myself, but here is the literature. Perhaps we can look at it together." People appreciated my honesty. It wasn't long before I had a customer--then two customers--and soon I was in business.

After some months, I joined a singles group called Theos, a term which means "to help each other spiritually" It was made up of Christian people who had lost their mates. I found it comforting to mingle with people who were battling the same pain I was.

One surprising revelation was the fact that nearly all of them had guilt feelings regarding their deceased mates. I felt guilty because I hadn't picked up on early signs that Esther was ill. Perhaps she then could have received the help of a physician sooner. When other survivors related their feelings of guilt to the group, I was surprised and relieved to discover that guilt was a normal part of the grieving process.

One member of the organization was Wilmadeen Kugler. We first got acquainted when we were assigned to the same discussion group. Thereafter, we saw each other several times, but neither of us was able to attend the meetings regularly. They were held in Grand Island, and it wasn't always handy to make the trip. Also, Wilmadeen was the farthest member, for she lived north of Bartlett on a ranch.

Comments by Wilmadeen:

In the summer of 1983, I went to Oklahoma to work for Wycliff Bible Translators. I mainly did secretarial work. When I returned to Nebraska, our Theos group was passing the word that members should write to Henry. He had been detained in the hospital with complications after surgery. Nearly everyone in our group wrote, including me.

I didn't know what to write except to relate what I had been doing over the summer. Since Henry had previously been in Oklahoma, he found my letter interesting. Our correspondence continued beyond his stay in the hospital.

I had been a widow since July 12, 1977, when my

husband, Wyvern Kugler, had been killed in a traffic accident. He was returning home after transporting a tank on a stack mover. A van approached from behind and began to pass. Unfortunately it didn't pull out quickly enough, and it hit the back left corner of the stack mover. The pressure on the tongue of the stack mover caused the tractor to jackknife. Wyvern was thrown out of the cab, and the tractor rolled on him.

"I have four children. At the time of Wyvern's death, the oldest, Peggy, was in North Platte working in a hospital. Mickee was married, and she and her husband was attending Bible School in Denver in preparation for the ministry. John, at eighteen, had graduated from high school. He had left home that week to help a friend with a construction project. Patricia was fifteen and had two more years of high school to complete.

"The neighbors congregated at our ranch and harvested our hay. John came home to help me clear up our business affairs and decide what to do with the cattle. He then went to Denver and got a job at a ski resort.

After Wyvern died, I rented the property and continued to teach school. John married in 1979, and Patricia and Peggy each married in 1980. Seven years of widowhood had come and gone, and with all the children settled elsewhere, I adjusted to being alone.

Henry continues: My children were ready for me to remarry before I was. Ruth Ann told me that she would feel it an honor to her mother if I remarried. "It would mean," she said, "that you and she got along together so well that you chose to marry again."

Once when Paul and Jamie were on furlough from the Navy, we were at a restaurant. There were several older ladies there. Paul said, "Are those ladies widows?"

"Yes," I answered.

He eyed me slyly. "Well-l-l--" he said, nudging me meaningfully with his elbow.

Wedding of Henry Cramer and Wilmadeen Kugler. June 30, 1984.

Wilmadeen and I decided to marry on June 30, 1984, but we had difficulty deciding on the location for the ceremony. Wilmadeen attended church in Chambers, a tiny town in north central Nebraska. I didn't know anyone in that town, and Wilmadeen didn't know anyone in Aurora. Finally we decided to be married in the little church on the grounds of the Stuhr Museum in Grand Island. All our children were able to attend except Mark who was in California and one of Wilmadeen's sons-in-law. Wilmadeen's daughter Mickee and her husband, Mike Neely, sang at our wedding.

We have a buggy that I got from a man in Dannebrog. A friend of mine, Harold Nachtigal, had a horse that I had trained for him. Without telling Wilmadeen, I asked him and his wife, Eunice, to bring the horse and buggy to Grand Island. After the marriage ceremony, I escorted Wilmadeen around in it. Later we enjoyed giving the grandchildren buggy rides. We went to the Holiday Inn for dinner.

We have enjoyed traveling. In 1985 and again in 1996 we flew to Germany to visit relatives. In 1988 we went to Peru to visit our friends in a jungle mission. We spent a couple of months each winter of the years '92, '93, and '94 at Rio Grande Bible Institute.

We lived on our acreage near Aurora, and I continued to sell feed. One year I was top salesman and won a fur coat for Wilmadeen. This year, 1997, I retired from selling feed, and we moved to a house in Aurora.

I enjoy my part-time job of driving a school bus.

I look around our home, noting our comfortable furniture, and our well stocked refrigerator. Outside, a car and a pickup are parked in the driveway. Am I the same person who, as a child, slept four in a bed on a straw mattress and cheered for hot chocolate and cookies on Hitler's birthday? Am I the German man who wore gunny sack clothes after the war? It is an amazement to me that I am here--a true citizen--accepted in spite of the evil deeds of Hitler.

I recall a time when we lived in Papillion, and our children went to Platteview School. The kids belonged to band and chorus, and we attended their musical presentations. At one program, Ruth Ann's class sang a rousing patriotic song. She stood proudly in the middle of the group and put her whole heart into the singing.

> *"This land is your land   This land is my land*
> *From California   To the New York Islands,"*

"Yes," I thought. "This land *is* my land, for incredibly, I am an American. But I have a lot of German in me, also, for I will never forget the place where I was born--my mother and dad--brothers and sisters--grandparents--the childhood friends who romped with me. I am forever part German as well as American." The beat of the song marched on:

> *"From redwood forests   To the Gulf Stream waters*
> *This land was made for you and me."**

Then as I watched Ruth Ann, my heart seemed to grow too large for my chest. My mind was filled with wonder. "There stands my own little girl, her every fiber projecting the sentiment in that song. Now there--there--is a *true* American!"

The End

**"This Land is Your Land"*, *by Woodie Guthrie. 1967.*

About the Author

Marie Kramer has lived in Nebraska all her life. She taught school in the Atkinson-Stuart area until her retirement in 1988. Since that time, she has enjoyed writing. *Heinrich to Henry* is the third book she has published.

The first book, *Homestead Fever*, 376 pages, is a collection of true pioneer stories which she gathered over the years from "old-timers" in Nebraska. The second, *Out of Barbed Wire into a Nazi Death March*, 150 pages, is a gripping account of three Nebraska men who were prisoners of war during World War II. After the publication of *Out of Barbed Wire*, additional World War II stories began to surface, for every community has men of retirement age who are now reviewing their lives and remembering their part in the war.

There are thousands of these stories to collect and record. *Heinrich to Henry* is one of them--but this particular account has a different focus. It is the story of a German soldier and his struggle to become an American.

To order books, write to Marie Kramer, York Mobile Plaza #20, York Nebraska 68467, or call 402-362-4357.

Homestead Fever, soft cover -- $10.00
Out of Barbed Wire, laminated -- $8.00
Heinrich to Henry, laminated -- $8.00

Add $3.00 to your order for postage/tax.

(Also, *Homestead Fever* is available in beautiful hard cover binding -- $16.00.)